# Love Match

## THE ART AND SCIENCE OF FINDING YOUR IDEAL RIGHT PARTNER

Shaelyn T. Pham, Ph.D.

Improve your life. Change your world.

Improve your life. Change your world.

Hatherleigh Press is committed to preserving and protecting the natural resources of the earth. Environmentally responsible and sustainable practices are embraced within the company's mission statement.

Visit us at www.hatherleighpress.com and register online for free offers, discounts, special events, and more.

Library of Congress Cataloging-in-Publication Data is available upon request.
ISBN: 978-1-57826-748-4

Interior Design by Cynthia Dunne

Printed in the United States
10 9 8 7 6 5 4 3 2 1

# CONTENTS

*To Jon Bopp, my partner in life. An incredibly loving, understanding, supportive and forgiving husband who shows me what true love looks like—unconditionally.*

# ACKNOWLEDGMENTS

I WANT TO thank my family and friends who continue to believe in me and have been supporting me with their encouragement and well wishes. I want to thank my creative team at Hatherleigh Press and editor, Ryan Kennedy, who helped make this book come alive. To my clients, who influenced and inspired me to write this book, thank you. I want to thank those of you who have picked up this book; I am honored to be a part of your journey.

This book would not be possible without the love and support I receive from my beloved husband, Jon Bopp.

And lastly, my amazing God, who has been there for every part of my journey and given me all that I need to help make a difference.

# INTRODUCTION

ONCE IN A lifetime, we're lucky enough to meet that one special person who captures our heart and touches our soul. Too often, this opportunity is missed, and we end up with nothing but memories of "the one that got away." We want to believe that it's poor timing, life circumstances, or that we just weren't ready due to our emotional hang-ups. Whatever the reason, we're left with pain and, possibly, regret.

We all want to go through life with a partner who is kind, loving, understanding, accepting, patient, and forgiving—someone that we can love, cherish, and count on for the rest of our life. But before we can have a romantic partner for life, we have to be open to love. When it comes to love and relationships, what we do consciously *and* what we do unconsciously matters. Some people, for example, recognize in themselves a tendency to sabotage their relationships, but they do not know why they do it or what is it they do to ruin their love affairs. Learning about ourselves and our attachment style is necessary, as it determines our approach to love and intimacy. This way, we can be in control of our love life instead of leaving it up to chance.

Even though we're created to be in relationships with one another, the first relationship we need to have is with ourselves. A few years ago, I published my first book, *The Joy of Me*, laying out the path to discovery for loving and living authentically. We need to have peace and harmony within ourselves before we can achieve that with another person and, ultimately, the world.

If you have read *The Joy of Me*, you might recall the infamous ex-boyfriend who wrote an inflammatory and unforgivable letter to my family after we broke up. I can understand that people lash out when they're hurt and angry—I could even ignore the verbal abuse, tolerate the destruction of property—but I didn't mention the cruel and unreasonable act of stealing my four-legged child, a fluffy off-white Pomeranian. It was a terrible time for me, but because all of his behavior was so visibly upsetting, it was much easier to move forward.

I know how it feels to fall in love and not be able to fall out of that toxic love. You're stuck in an unpredictable and unstable relationship. This kind of love leaves you feeling confused, frustrated, and unable to move on. You believe that you've found your soulmate—you can see the person at their core and connect with their soul—but you don't know how fix the sporadic cycle of breaking up and getting back together. Each time you go back, your heart gets broken again. This is periodical love, and it can never satisfy your hunger or quench your thirst.

The journey to find the love of my life wasn't exactly filled with roses and rainbows, which is why I felt I had to write this book. I do consider myself a hopeless romantic, albeit with a practical view. I want to share with you what I've learned along the way, in dating as well as in marriage, so that you don't have to repeat my mistakes. I'd also like to share the expertise and knowledge that I have used to help the countless clients I've worked with over the years.

I don't want you to get stuck in the vicious cycle of pain and never-ending disappointment. I don't want you to lose your hope and trust in love and romance. I don't want you to feel more jaded or lug your baggage from relationship to relationship. I want you to have your true love, and a healthy relationship by building a solid foundation so it can weather any storm.

True love is not just a fairy tale or Hollywood fiction. It is real and tangible. I'm more in love with my husband today than the day we were married. Our relationship has more depth, understanding, love, compassion, fun, and security as each day passes, and you can have it, too. I'm delighted to take this journey with you and show you the road map on how to achieve it!

[ 1 ]

# The Preparation

Destiny is not a matter of chance; it is a matter
of choice. It is not a thing to be waited for, it is
a thing to be achieved.

—WILLIAM JENNINGS BRYAN

LIFE IS AN adventure filled with unknowns.

When we take a journey or go on a holiday getaway, it requires
preparation. Even as a spontaneous traveler, while you may not
have your itinerary mapped out, you still have an idea of where
you're going. What's more, the length of your trip determines
how you prepare. If you were to take a three-week vacation, for
example, you'd prepare for it differently than for a two-day "stay-
cation."

Even the simplest things, like taking a holiday adventure, require us to make preparations. Yet when it comes to love, we all

too often leave it to chance. We hope that we'll meet someone, and if we are lucky, we'll find each other attractive and have chemistry. Then we'll fall in love and somehow, magically, it will work out, and we'll have a partner for life.

I'm sorry to say it, but the probability of that happening is slim. You *are* going to need to put some work in to be happy in love for the rest of your life. So, let's start looking at the basics of what you need to have in your travel bag to prepare for the arrival of your true love.

## WHAT DO YOU WANT FROM A PARTNER? HAVE YOU THOUGHT ABOUT IT?

If you have, that's great. If you haven't, now is a good time to think about your "must haves" and "must *not* haves." I want you to think of three of each; there can be more than three, but limiting yourself to three of each forces you to prioritize what's significant for you. It also helps you to focus and not be distracted by what's not important, especially if you have anxiety about commitment. The longer your checklist, the harder it is to find someone who meets all the requirements, giving you the perfect excuse to run away.

It is necessary to know who we are and what we want. By examining our values and how important they are to us, we're able to determine what is negotiable and what is not. In the beginning, we value having common interests and look for them in a prospective partner. Sometimes we're also willing to change who we are to please our potential partner ... but to what degree?

*Michelle*
Michelle is a busy neurosurgeon who does not respect men, and she knows that about herself. She doesn't believe that a man

could truly add any value to her life. She is young, beautiful, and successful; whatever she wants, she gets herself. She is open to dating, but has not been open to working on a relationship. She states that she hasn't found a man who makes her *want* to work for it. Recently, she found a man who is on par with her and even more headstrong. She is smitten by him.

"It is a breath of fresh air," she said, "to have an alpha man who doesn't let me get away with things. That's the problem with all the guys I have dated in the past. It was good in the beginning, and then, over time, I'd just walk all over them like a door mat." Devin has no problem being assertive, taking the lead, making plans, and even telling her what to wear. She loves it when he makes plans and tells her exactly what to do. She has no problem when he started wanting her to wear more dresses, high heels, red lipstick, and be "sexier," because she wants to look good for him. He wanted her to grow out her hair, which she did. And then one day, he wanted her "to be how a woman should be—in the kitchen, cooking for her man."

Michelle doesn't have a problem with being in the kitchen; as a matter of fact, she enjoys cooking in her free time. However, she has worked hard to be where she is and doesn't want a man to tell her what her place is in life. Her father did that, telling her mother her place in life was in the house, cooking, cleaning, and taking care of the kids. Though Michelle expressed appreciation for having had a stay-at-home mother, she also saw how miserable her mom was.

This is when Michelle and I had lengthy discussions about her values: what is important to her, what she is willing to give, where she wants to grow, and at what point Devin will accept her for who she is. The hope is that he'll see her as being good enough to love without trying to mold and shape her to his liking.

Cooking was not the issue. What was more important in this

situation is that Michelle feels like she keeps coming up short after a period of dating. Devin asked her to make a change, and she obliged. But it was her values that helped her realize that if she keeps giving, he'll keep asking. Her whole life, spent trying to gain her parents' approval, has now been replaced by a man's. She needs to be true to herself, live authentically, and believe that she is good enough.

Having had the privilege of working with individuals and couples over the past decade, I've noticed that there are recurring themes and issues. Sex and money are some of the hottest topics, and we'll talk more in detail about them later.

**At this moment, I invite you to put down this book, grab a pen or pencil, and answer the following basic questions using this scale:**

**1–Not Important; 2–Somewhat Important; 3–Indifferent; 4–Important; 5 – Very Important**

__ How important is it for me to be in a two-income relationship? If so, what is the necessary level of income my partner needs to earn?

__ How important is it for me to have a partner sharing my faith?

__ How important is it for me to have kids? If so, how many?

__ Who will raise the kids? (i.e., mom/dad stays at home, day care, nanny, etc.?)

__ Is it important for me to marry someone of the same faith? If it's not important and I'm in an interfaith relationship, whose faith will the kids be raised in?

＿ How do I feel about having my in-laws or my parents stay with us? Why?

＿ How open does my prospective partner have to be?

＿ How much effort do I need to see my prospective partner putting into our relationship?

＿ How flexible am I with the issues raised in these questions?

If there are more values and qualities that are important to you, continue with this format and rate them using this scale.

This is important information to have in your back pocket when you're dating someone but aren't necessarily committed. Remember, as we learn and grow wiser, we do change our minds. When we love someone, we also change, not because we have to, but because we want to be a better version of ourselves. Ideally, your potential partner also wants to be the best version of themselves. *That* is the key; a person has to be open to growth. If you're growing and changing while your partner remains stagnant, you might grow apart, which might lead to you leaving them. However, don't go into a relationship with the idea that you can change people for the better or persuade them to change to prove how much they love you.

## MEETING OF THE HEARTS

The dream of changing a bad boy into faithfully loving you and *only* you, ever popular during your teenage years, doesn't necessarily stop when you reach adulthood, unless you're conscientious of it. In adulthood, the temptation of the chase is much subtler. He's not an outright bad boy, and you may not be a good girl, but the need for a chase, the desire to "tame" him, remains. This is a dangerous recipe for girls who are Chasers (we'll discuss this archetype in greater detail later on). The idea of being able to tame a bad boy or a man who has a strong hold on his heart and have him give it up to you can make a girl feel very special and significant—he's changing for you and only you. Who wouldn't feel invincible with that kind of power?

The truth of the matter is that the chase will be fruitlessly relentless and, if I may dare to say, unnatural. Right or wrong, most of us have a tendency to value what we work hard for. When you're too ready to give your heart away, the other person may not feel deserving of it because they haven't earned it. But courtship is a demonstration of wooing one another and showing one's willingness to put in the effort for each other to build a relationship. When one is willing to work *for* a relationship, then one is open to work *at* a relationship in the long run.

You may think this is a game that everyone should play when it comes to dating, but it isn't; it's simply a method of pattern and prediction, as well as an optimization of one of our biological needs. There are many other needs that we need to be aware of when it comes to dating and intimacy.

## THE FOUR TYPES OF INTIMACY

The essential part of preparation is knowing more about yourself and knowing what you're looking for in a partner. When asked, "What are you looking for in a partner?" ninety-nine percent of the time I hear, "Someone I can have a stimulating conversation with," or "Someone with a sense of humor."

I'm not surprised by these answers; these characteristics are forms of intimacy. Oftentimes, when people hear the word *intimacy*, they think of physical intimacy—sex. But that's only one form of intimacy. There are four different types: *physical intimacy* is the most easily recognized and includes anything from sensual touches to sexual intercourse; *intellectual intimacy* comes from sharing thoughts and ideas, and can be expressed and enjoyed by sharing similarities and differences of opinions; *emotional intimacy* comes from comfortably sharing your feelings and from empathizing with someone else; and *experiential intimacy* is the spending of time and sharing of activities together.

## Jayden

Let's take a look at Jayden and see how these different kinds of intimacy play out in real life. Jayden, a highly educated young man, received his doctorate degree from MIT. You may have conjured up an image of him in your head; perhaps you see someone with thick glasses, his shirt tucked into his khaki pants, possibly nerdy-looking, with slightly disheveled hair. Au contraire—Jayden is tall, has a good build, and is quite handsome. He does consider himself socially awkward, however, which has affected his dating life. He rarely gets a second date.

"Come to think of it, I barely make it through the first date," he relates. "I can't seem to hold a conversation. I don't like small talk. 'What do you do for a living?' 'What do you do for fun?' I answer the questions, of course, but with the number of first dates I have gone through, you can imagine how it feels."

"Like an interview," I empathized.

He nods.

"So, what do you like to talk about?" I inquired.

"There are so many things. The last thing she read that got her thinking, what's going on with the world … the war? What about technology and how it's impacting our lives or lack thereof?" he said.

As you may have noticed, Jayden is more comfortable connecting on the intellectual level. When he's not able to make that connection, he quickly eliminates the prospect. Therefore, he's not able to move forward in a relationship or have any type of intimacy.

Jayden came to realize his "social awkwardness" is due to the limitations involved in solely relying on his cognitive abilities. Fortunately, he was open to making changes. For his following date, instead of drinks and dinner, I suggested he give experiential intimacy a try. He and his date might do something more casual during the day, like go-carting, bike riding on the beach, paddle boarding, or even taking in a baseball game or some other such activity.

Jayden came back with an update—he had a great time. By the end of the bike ride on the boardwalk, he was feeling more comfortable. He was able to joke, laugh, and let his guard down. What he didn't realize was that while he criticized small talk, he did much the same thing, but on a more intellectual level. When he doesn't feel pressure to put on a show, he is more relaxed and can just be himself. He is actually more dynamic than he lets on; he's not just "one note."

"I'm actually looking forward to our second date," he told me. "It's this Wednesday. I'm attracted to her, and we seem to have chemistry. I didn't kiss her, but I'll let you know how it goes," he said with a mischievous smile.

Intellectual intimacy is still important to Jayden. He wants to have someone who is able to intellectually challenge him. He's excited when a woman is quick-witted. At the very least, he wants a woman who is able to hold a pleasant and stimulating exchange. However, he's no longer making intellectual intimacy his only choice when approaching women.

Like Jayden, most of us tend to go into new situations with the style of intimacy that we're most comfortable with and most confident in. However, not everyone is the same, and different people value different forms of intimacy in varying degrees.

Jayden has spent most of his life using his head, dealing with logic and reason. It was not a surprise for me to find out that emotional intimacy was the most difficult form of intimacy for him and the last thing he could open up to. For Jayden, the order of intimacies that he was most comfortable and confident sharing went something like this: intellectual, experiential, physical, and then emotional. When it comes to intellectual intimacy, he's well versed; this is when he believes that he is at his best, like a peacock about to do his dance. As far as emotional intimacy goes, that is too invasive and personal for him. He has to feel comfortable and trusting enough to let people in.

## WHAT IS YOUR PREFERRED INTIMACY?

When I ask my male clients to tell me their preferred intimacy, I often get a follow-up question: "It's great that I know mine, but if I need to impress a girl I'm interested in, do I need to know hers?" Some of my male clients have also joked that, "Maybe I don't need to know mine. I just need to know hers, and then I just go in with the approach that she likes."

They make a good point, but though the approach is clever, it's also essentially a deception if you can't sustain it for a lifetime. While you may give your prospective partner the impression that you're a perfect match, you're actually depriving yourself of your needs if their intimacy type isn't your preferred form. Intimacy is not just a way to connect on dates; it's the steel support that holds up the relationship. Therefore, you don't want to build the foundation of a relationship on lies. It is as important to know your own preferred form of intimacy as it is to know your partner's. That way, both of your desires can be met.

There is a wonderful way of getting that information while you're still trying to get to know the other person—ask. Ask the other person to help you prepare for your date together. Usually, when you ask someone, "What do you prefer to do on a date?" or "What is a perfect date to you?" their answers can give you some general ideas. When you know what they like, you can take that into consideration, while remaining mindful of your preferred intimacy style, as well.

When you're authentic and open for new experiences, you may be surprised at what comes your way. But not everyone is prepared to get what they ask for.

### Kayla

Kayla is a client who I now see when needed. She initially came to see me because she was having problems with her boyfriend. We worked on her, but unfortunately her relationship didn't make it. As she was growing and learning to love herself, she realized that he was not the man for her because he wasn't open to changing and growing.

Even though she initiated the breakup, it was still painful. We worked through the breakup, looking to help her process the doubt of her decision. We discussed her thinking of getting back together with him. Eventually, we came to a place of acceptance and gracefully moving forward. We spent a good amount of time working on her self-esteem, and she is finally at a place where she is no longer settling on getting together with a man she would have to "fix."

After a time, Kayla met another man at a business mixer. He was down-to-earth and not pretentious. For their first date, they went to a baseball game together. She met a couple of his friends at the game, and she had a great time. After the game, they went out for a drink, which gave them an opportunity to talk. He even followed up with her to make plans for the following weekend.

For all the time that I have known her, Kayla has wanted

someone who would take the initiative with planning so she wouldn't have to do it. She wanted someone she could talk to about her emotions, unlike her ex-boyfriend. More importantly, she wanted someone who was active and communicative. She has gone on several dates with this new man in her life, and so far, he fits every requirement. However, she is hesitant about him because he presented her with a list of activities that they could do for their next date. That's too much for her; he's too eager. His downfall is that he's too excited to see her.

Kayla's *love language* (discussed in more detail in Chapter 7) is quality time. However, she thinks it's problematic that this new man wants to do all of these activities instead of having dates that involve lengthy conversations over dinner. It is worth mentioning that she has gone through many conversational dinner dates and usually just dreads them!

When we processed through her hesitation, we found the real problem was her fear. She couldn't believe that she'd already found love and was afraid that there might be a chance she would get hurt, so she looked for reasons to turn him away.

Preparation is not just knowing more about yourself and what you want in a relationship; after all, the who, how, and when we meet the love of our lives can be unpredictable. As the Roman philosopher Seneca put it, "Luck is what happens when preparation meets opportunity." Love is the same way; but when it comes to love, it's not about being at the right place at the right time for that opportunity, it's about being open and ready for it. You have to be open to accept what you have always wanted when it comes. You must both put in the effort to create a meaningful relationship.

The more prepared you are, the greater chance you'll have of finding your true love.

# The Science of Love

The meeting of two personalities is like the
contact of two chemical substances: if there is
any reaction, both are transformed.

—C.G. Jung

*Christy*
"I think I'm falling in love!" Christy exclaimed.

I came to know Christy recently when we began meeting once
a week for her individual therapy. She came to see me to deal
with the estranged relationship she had with her father. Her parents divorced when she was fifteen, and now, in her mid-twen-
ties, she wants to have a relationship with her father. A part of
her really wants to have him walk her down the aisle on her
wedding day.

"How do you know that you're in love?" I asked.

Christy named the physical symptoms such as butterflies in her stomach, sweaty palms, and the fact that she couldn't stop thinking about him. He's the first thought she has waking up in the morning and the last thought before falling asleep at night.

She continued to gush over her feelings for him. I patiently listened to her, and I could see it on her face. When she talks about this man, she lights up like a Christmas tree with an uncontrollable grin from ear to ear. Christy feels like she is on top of the world. Nothing is impossible, and no one can ruin it for her. She feels empowered.

The amazing thing about love is that it gives us such an incredible feeling, the belief that we can climb mountains and cross vast seas to be with that one person. With feelings like that, it is natural for us to want to be in love and to be loved.

We're created to be in relationships with one another. Finding this new man gives Christy hope that there is someone wonderfully made just for her. He is the opposite of her father; attentive to her needs and concerned about her well-being. He's also funny and constantly tries to make her laugh. He makes her feel like a princess.

As a relational being, Christy is no different from anyone else. We all want to have that one special person to grow old with. It is not necessarily because we're scared of being alone or need to have a partner, but because life is better when you have a significant other to share all of the beautiful moments it has to offer.

Is love supposed to be magical? Are there fireworks when you first kiss? Does time stop and does the world stand still when you're in each other's arms?

There is nothing wrong with wanting to see fireworks or having time stand still when you're with your true love. True love certainly does exist, but it's not exactly like what we see in the movies. What we see in the movies is the final product. What we don't see in the movies are the thousands of behind-the-scenes, uncut, and unedited moments. Don't be fooled into thinking that love is like what you see in the movies. It's not quick and easy. When you see a happy, lively couple with a passionate relationship, know that countless hours are being invested behind closed doors. They work hard to make it incredible.

## WHAT IS LOVE?

For thousands of years, humans have professed the beauty of love, but I don't think we have come to agree on one universal definition of what love is.

When I told my friend, Toni, a musician, that I'm writing a book on love, he introduced me to this beautiful song called "No Sé Estar Enamorado," by Jarabe de Palo.

I don't know Spanish, so I had him translate it for me. This is what the song says:

> *When it comes to love, I only know I know nothing.*
> *When it comes to love, I only know there's nothing I know.*
> *Talking about love, it's so difficult to know.*
> *When you're in love, and without you, I would die.*

Is this what being in love is all about? A tragic pain and the inability to survive on the other side of the coin? I'm certain that is not every case—especially in the case of "true love."

## WHAT IS "TRUE LOVE"? IS IT JUST A FEELING?

The wonderful news is that love isn't just a fleeting feeling of elation. It is the comfort of feeling safe and securely connected to another being when you're at your most vulnerable— knowing that you *could* get hurt, but believing that your partner *would not* do so. It's during these most vulnerable moments that intimacy is formed, and intimacy is the core of true love.

Before getting into the emotional intelligence of intimacy and love, let's first examine the chemistry behind love. Let's look at what science has to say about love and the effect of this chemical-inducing and brain-altering phenomenon that creates sleepless nights for many people.

## WHERE DOES ATTRACTION COME FROM?

Science has deconstructed the feeling of attraction and explained the chemistry behind romantic feelings of love. I should warn you that knowing the science behind it can be a bit of a disappointment; it takes away the mystery and romantic fantasy of what we envision falling in love to be like.

There are a number of chemicals responsible for a person falling in love. As science explains it, physical attraction begins with sight and is purely based on the person's appearance; in a split second, the brain determines whether the person is "hot" or "not." This is followed by another determination about the person's voice and scent. When you like what you see, smell, and hear, this triggers the release of chemicals in your brain such as dopamine and norepinephrine. These chemicals are responsible for communicating excitement and happiness through certain physical symptoms; for example, increased heart rate, flushed skin, and even perspiration. As you get closer to each other and display more physical affection, dopamine keeps getting released. When dopamine levels are optimal, it decreases the level of cortisol, which is a stress hormone. Hence, your stress level is low when you're engaged in physical intimacy. As affection increases with hugging, kissing, cuddling, and sexual encounters, it releases and elevates oxytocin, which is a love hormone. When people are in love, they also have low levels of serotonin. Low levels of serotonin can cause obsessive-compulsive tendencies, which explains the uncontrollable thoughts you have of your loved one all day long.

## Why Does Attraction Occur with Certain People and Not Others?

I'll bet there are times when you recognize someone as handsome or beautiful, like their voice, and even like their scent, but still don't feel attracted to them. You may even verbalize this with "He's not my type," or "I'm not interested in her."

Generally speaking, when it comes to chemistry and connection, we tend to be drawn to people who share similar types of intimacy or personality traits that we exhibit and like within ourselves. Likewise, when there are traits that we dislike within ourselves, whether we are conscious of it or not, these get magnified when looking at others. We consciously look for traits that we admire or would like to possess ourselves. Finally, the psyche looks for the missing piece of the puzzle to complement our unconscious needs. For example, if you have a tendency to be clingy and needy, you'll be attracted to a person who has the need to *be* needed.

Helen Fisher, an anthropologist who has spent her time studying the brain chemistry associated with love, believes this has to do with personality traits. Based on the four chemicals that are regularly associated with personality traits, she came up with four personality types and the role of these personalities in attraction.

## The Four Personality Types

The first personality type is the *Explorer*, which is linked to dopamine. As it sounds, the Explorer is adventurous and spontaneous.

You optimistically seek new and novel experiences. You tend to be curious and creative. However, you are very susceptible to boredom and can be impulsive. As you are more energized by external stimuli, you tend to look outward instead of within yourself, which can lead to a lack of introspection.

Another chemical is serotonin, which expresses the sociability of the *Builder*. You tend to be popular. As a Builder, you are calm and exhibit self-control. You tend to be more traditional and can be religious. You're conscientious of rules and social norms. You can have the need to rigidly follow and adhere to plans at times. You also have a tendency to be more cautious, which explains your need to be more detailed-oriented.

The *Director*, the third personality type, is considered to be more analytical and tough-minded. You are direct and decisive. This type of personality is associated with testosterone. Your ambition and competitiveness can make you have an extreme sensitivity to rank. However, you tend to be less socially aware and have less emotional recognition and empathy for others.

The fourth personality type is an expression of estrogen and oxytocin—the *Negotiator*. As a Negotiator, you are imaginative and able to see the big picture. You are intuitive and understand the emotions of others, helping you to be more compassionate. You have mental flexibility, which can make you too agreeable.

Who we are attracted to depends on our own personality type. Builders and Explorers tend to attract people with the same personality type as themselves, whereas Directors and Negotiators tend to attract each other, as they complement one another. Whether we are consciously looking for a partner with common interests, similar physical, psychological, and emotional traits, or someone who is different to complement our needs, there is still another element that must be taken into consideration. When we approach love, we're not only presenting our innate natures, we are also toting our baggage from our childhood—that is, how we were nurtured in our environment—which shapes how we fall in love. So, by knowing ourselves and what we want on the conscious as well as unconscious level, we will have a better chance at being successful in finding our true love.

Knowing all that we know about chemistry and love, there is still mystery in love. A lot of the mystery is in the work of the unconscious. The more you know about your unconscious attraction, the better your chance of having the love of your life and a healthy relationship.

The great news is that the unconscious can be brought into consciousness. In this book, we will go into depth about the unconscious to help you bring what is living in the dark into the light. In this way, you'll be able to find your *soulmate*—someone who is suitable for you and who you are compatible with—so that you can build a lifelong, dream relationship and have a passionate marriage.

# [ 3 ]

# *True Love and Soulmate Love*

> Every heart sings a song, incomplete, until another heart whispers back. Those who wish to sing always find a song. A touch of lover, everyone becomes a poet.
>
> —PLATO

## WHAT IS TRUE LOVE?

If you believe the story of Adam and Eve, then you believe that Eve was made from one of Adam's ribs. What the story insinuates is that there is one person who is made specifically for us and that person is destined to be our soulmate. Many people also interpret that a rib was chosen because it symbolizes that the two need to walk side by side as partner, not one ahead leading or following behind the other.

Is it through this soulmate that we'll find true love? Have you ever questioned the idea of true love or soulmate love? Is your true love or soulmate the one you end up with for life? What if you get divorced? Or your significant other passes away and you remarry? Does that mean the first partner was not your true love? What about "the one that got away?" Could that person have been your true love?

One person I dated told me that your true love is your soulmate, who you love with all of your heart, at all times, for the rest of your life. I must admit that this is a very sweet thought. However, being a psychologist, I have couples telling me how much they despise each other; that's why they're in my office. Some of the couples are not able to get along with each other; they can't find a rhythm that works for them, and they're just not happy together.

There are various reasons for these feelings. Some of the partners feel suffocated, controlled, hurt, misunderstood, or unloved, which leads to a lot of insecurity and resentment. Some of these couples feel that they're with the wrong person, so coming to therapy is their way of trying to fix the situation—or, to be more accurate, have me figure out what's wrong with the other person and fix them. Then, if (or when) the person is not "fixable," leaving is warranted. This helps them feel less guilty moving forward as they tell themselves that they tried everything they could to save the relationship. Of course, not everyone coming into my office thinks that way. A lot of them genuinely want to work on their relationship to stay with their loved one.

### Terri and Richard

Terri sits at the opposite end of the couch with tears in her eyes. "He is my soulmate. I want to be with him for the rest of my life. I think he would be a great husband and father. We have talked about this. I want to build our lives together and have a family someday. We were so good together at one point, but I don't know what happened," Terri confessed.

I believe that your soulmate is the person you choose, so long as that person also chooses you. If the person *doesn't* choose you, then that person is not your soulmate. In this chapter, I'll show you why having true love is as simple as that—and yet at the same time, as difficult as climbing Mt. Everest. I'll attempt to answer the question of "What happened?" in Terri's situation, and why it is simple—but not easy—to mend a relationship.

## THE DIFFERENT STAGES OF A RELATIONSHIP

A relationship is a living organism. Relationships change, just like seasons. You can't force summer to stay longer, nor delay autumn from coming. You have to learn to enjoy the season as it presents itself and be appreciative in order to make the best of it. The sun is just as necessary as the rain to bring cherry blossoms in the spring. Your relationship—every relationship—has its own dynamics.

There are four different stages in a relationship that every couple must go through to achieve happiness. The first stage is independence. This is when you are two people independent of each other. You're a fierce individual with your own plan and intention. Your comings and goings are solely yours, without commitment or obligations to another person. Your every decision is simply to attend to your own wants, needs, and general well-being.

The second stage is dependence. This is also the beginning of a romantic relationship, and is considered the best stage of the relationship for many. It's a fair assumption for me to say that you've probably already known the best stage of a relationship.

It's on the tip of everyone's tongue—the *honeymoon phase*. It denotes the most beautiful and exciting stage of your relationship. In this stage of a relationship, you're dependent on each other for happiness. You want to depend on and want to be depended on by your partner. It gives you a great sense of joy to be the source of happiness for your partner.

When Terri says, "We were so in love," she is referring to this "honeymoon phase" of their relationship. It's the *dependent stage* when your livelihood seemingly rests on each other. You're joined at the hip. Honeymooners tend to be inseparable from each other. In this initial stage, you give each other your best and see only the best in your partner. You want to put the other person's needs first. You want to do everything you possibly can to make your partner's life easier and happier. You're inseparable because you don't want to be away from one another. Each second apart seems like a century, and you simply can't get enough of each other.

This honeymoon period lasts for a while, anywhere between six months to two years. You're madly in love, and nothing matters, so long as you have each other. No obstacle is too big to overcome. You'll fight for each other. It is the mantra of the two of you against the world, and it may feel like you can live on love alone.

Most people expect relationships to stay this way, forever blissful. Unfortunately, much as you are the breath of fresh air to each other, that breath of oxygen eventually turns into carbon dioxide. It requires you to exhale before it becomes poisonous.

This takes us into the third stage of a relationship. It is a difficult stage for most couples. Many struggle to accept the natural course of change in a relationship. The majority of us fight to hold onto the honeymoon phase for as long as we can. Some try to move past it but can't, which leads to arguments and disappointment. Thus, they end up in the vicious cycle of code-pendency and losing parts of themselves. You don't have to lose yourself to gain a relationship. Your love is meant to enhance who you are as a person, not deplete your sense of identity.

A great example of this codependency or symbiotic relationship is a mother and her newborn. They're attached to each other by the umbilical cord. Even after it is cut, they're still very much dependent on each other; the baby is physically dependent on its mother, and the mother is enamored by and in love with her baby. The baby becomes her world and she emotionally loses herself in her baby. But naturally, babies grow and learn to crawl, walk, run, and to be less completely dependent on their mother. They want to explore their environment, which separates them from their mother. But that doesn't mean the baby no longer cares for or loves their mother. The baby still adores her and will come back to her.

This separation also happens in relationships. However, most couples see this progression as a sign that something is wrong with the relationship. When reality sets in, there may be differences between the two of you; for example, you may have different hobbies and interests. When one person is holding on to the dependency and the other is pulling away, trying to regain one's sense of self, it often leaves the other person feeling uncared for. We also have a tendency of personalizing and making it about us. We may interpret this natural pulling away to mean that they want breathing room because they want to get away from us. But two-year-old children will run toward a playground when they see one. They run because they want to play. They want to be independent. It has nothing to do with their mothers. They're not trying to get away from mom. Ideally, they know that they can freely run to play and return to their mothers anytime and their mothers won't be upset with them.

This is where Teri and Richard are; they are practicing their crawling. They're exploring the landscape of their relationship as well as their own sense of identity. Terri is fighting to stay in the honeymoon phase, and Richard is trying to move into the *independent phase*. During the dependent stage of their relationship, they were happy to oblige and do what it took to make their partner happy. Now, they feel obligated and resentful of having to take care of each other's happiness. They have been together for two and a half years. Their relationship was great in the beginning. They still want to get married and have a family, but they don't think it is possible the way it is. They want to know if their relationship can be salvaged or if they should move on.

There are a number of couples who successfully make it through this stage and on into the next one. However, many do get stuck in this vicious cycle of fighting to stay together but needing space from each other. They want independence but are emotionally dependent. They want freedom, but stay in restriction. They want commitment, but end up with obligations. When it gets too vicious to bear, they end up breaking it off and moving on to someone else, hoping it will be better.

I asked them both, "In your opinion, what do you think the problem is?"

"He's changed," Terri responded.

"She's controlling," he snapped back.

"How has he changed?" I asked.

"I don't know. He used to be really sweet," Teri answered.

"That's because you weren't controlling me," Richard cut in.

Terri is an independent young woman. She has her own life—hobbies, family, friends, and a career. She was attracted to Richard because he was also very independent. He has a good head on his shoulders. He's driven in his career and has a great group of friends. She admires how well put together he is.

They met each other through a mutual friend, who set them up on a date after Terri broke up with her then-boyfriend of two years. He had cheated on her; in fact, several of her ex-boyfriends had cheated on her. She was terrified and heartbroken each time, but she picked herself up, dusted herself off, and, being a courageous woman, put herself out there again. However, each time she gets a new guy, she tightens the leash a bit. It's fine in the beginning because she doesn't need to do that much, as they hang out with each other most of the time. But as time goes by, her tight grip gets more noticeable. And she is doing the same thing with Richard now.

"I can't even hang out with my friends without being interrogated by her," he complains.

"That's because you lie," she whines.

It hasn't always been this way. Richard was very accommodating at first; he didn't mind cutting back his time with his friends. He also slowly cut back on activities he did alone. He engaged in more of the "us" activities, and he was happy to do so, at first. But whenever he wanted to hang out with the guys, conflicts arose. They'd argue, they'd fight, she'd cry. And then he'd stay at home comforting her, but the comforting eventually stopped. As time went on, he would just get upset, she would end up in the bedroom, and he would spend the evening in the living room. So instead of having to put up with more fights, it was just easier for Richard to have more "work meetings."

I'm not condoning or excusing Richard's behavior, but his reasoning was, "I didn't want to fight anymore. I'm not doing anything wrong; I'm just tired of fighting." To avoid fighting and to keep the peace, he continued to lie, but then he got caught.

Terri keeps tab on Richard's schedule. It gives her a sense of security knowing his whereabouts. She believes if he only engages in activities that involve her, then he can't talk to other women, which means he can't flirt and cheat.

"You can't stop him if he wants to cheat," I pointed out.

Richard nods in agreement. "You couldn't stop your exes from cheating on you."

To which I add, "Also, don't you want him to be with you because he wants to, instead of shackling him?"

She sheepishly agrees.

Successfully navigating through this *codependent dynamic* requires a number of things. It requires you to practice stepping out of your comfort zone. You need to accept the fact that your partner may find other people attractive; that doesn't mean your partner is going to cheat. Attraction is uncontrollable, whereas cheating is controllable; it's a choice. And honest communication is a must. You need to recognize that you can't fulfill all of your partner's needs, no matter how great you are at wearing different hats and taking on different roles. You need to have respect for your partner to take care of their own needs. Otherwise, you'd have to be responsible for their happiness; a task that I'm certain anyone would fail at. You also need to respect your own happiness and focus on what you once did as an independent person. This way, you're in charge of your own happiness. You can't make your happiness someone else's responsibility. Otherwise, your partner will fail and disappoint you. Going back to the example of children and their mother, children have to learn and practice to do things for themselves, and eventually become independent of their parents as adults. Generally speaking, it is not healthy for adult children to depend on their parents. This practice exemplifies the need for us to do the same in a relationship. We have to learn to operate independently so we don't become codependent on each other.

When you're able to do this, you're a step closer to having a healthy relationship.

It also requires courage, as it leaves you feeling vulnerable. It requires the willingness to change the pattern of the relationship, breaking old ways and habits of relating to one another. While doing this, it forces us to face our own insecurity, whatever it may be, that has hindered the relationship from blossoming.

As for Terri and Richard, we started breaking down their symbiotic, or codependent, relationship patterns. They needed to know that they came together by choice—because they wanted to, not by force. I had each of them fill up their schedule with their own activities, hobbies, and interests. They needed to plan out their schedule exactly how they want it, excluding each other, since they need to regain their own individuality in the relationship. Then, I had them pick out two days of the week that they would like to see each other. This is quality time intentionally set aside for each other. This is necessary for them to stay connected while trying to be independent. They had to discuss and agree on the two days that work best for both of them. Through this discussion and negotiation, they learned more about each other's needs. They came to recognize and understand the importance of their own needs and their partner's. They learned to take care of their own needs instead of depending on their partner to fulfill them. They also learn to appreciate the undivided attention they give each other in their precious time together.

The tougher part was when they were apart doing their own activities. For several months, we were going back and forth, up and down, like a roller coaster. Some weeks were easier than others. There were times when they felt motivated and excited; other times, they slipped and failed miserably. As the saying goes, "most things are easier said than done," so I had to remind them that's why it's also called a "practicing phase." It's the *practice* of being independent or *differentiated* in a relationship. In this practice stage, you either work to move into differentiation, or you'll remain in a codependent relationship where you struggle to find independency and an intimate connection.

Below is a Differentiation of Self Inventory that I invite you to take to see where you are emotionally. When you know your level of emotional differentiation from your family, you'll be able to better relate with others, particularly your partner in a relationship. Your level of emotional differentiation shapes your way of connecting to your partner.

Directions: These are questions concerning your thoughts and feelings about yourself and relationships with others. Please read each statement carefully and decide how much the statement is generally true of you on a 1 (not at all) to 6 (very) scale. If you believe that an item does not pertain to you (e.g., you are not currently married or in a committed relationship, or one or both of your parents are deceased), please answer the item according to your best guess about what your thoughts and feelings would be in that situation. Be sure to answer every item, and try to be as honest and accurate as possible in your responses.

| | |
|---|---|
| 1. People have remarked that I'm overly emotional. | 1 2 3 4 ⑤ 6 |
| 2. I have difficulty expressing my feelings to people I care for. | 1 2 3 4 5 ⑥ |
| 3. I often feel inhibited around my family. | 1 2 3 ④ 5 6 |
| 4. I tend to remain pretty calm, even under stress. | 1 2 3 ④ 5 6 |
| 5. I'm likely to smooth over or settle conflicts between two people whom I care about. | 1 2 3 4 ⑤ 6 |

| | |
|---|---|
| 6. When someone close to me disappoints me, I withdraw from him or her for a time. | 1 2 3 ④ 5 6 |
| 7. No matter what happens in my life, I know that I'll never lose my sense of who I am. | 1 2 3 ④ 5 6 |
| 8. I tend to distance myself when people get too close to me. | 1 2 3 4 ⑤ 6 |
| 9. It has been said (or could be said) of me that I am still very attached to my parent(s). | 1 2 3 4 5 ⑥ |
| 10. I wish that I weren't so emotional. | 1 2 3 ④ 5 6 |
| 11. I usually do not change my behavior simply to please another person. | 1 ② 3 4 5 6 |
| 12. My spouse or partner could not tolerate it if I were to express to him or her my true feelings about some things. | 1 2 3 ④ 5 6 |
| 13. Whenever there is a problem in my relationship, I'm anxious to get it settled right away. | 1 2 3 4 ⑤ 6 |
| 14. At times my feelings get the best of me and I have trouble thinking clearly. | 1 ② 3 4 5 6 |
| 15. When I am having an argument with someone, I can separate my thoughts about the issue from my feelings about the person. | 1 2 ③ 4 5 6 |
| 16. I'm often uncomfortable when people get too close to me. | 1 2 3 4 5 ⑥ |
| 17. It's important for me to keep in touch with my parents regularly. | 1 2 3 4 5 ⑥ |
| 18. At times, I feel as if I'm riding an emotional roller coaster. | 1 2 3 4 ⑤ 6 |
| 19. There's no point in getting upset about things I cannot change. | 1 2 3 4 ⑤ 6 |

| | |
|---|---|
| 20. I'm concerned about losing my independence in intimate relationships. | 1 2 3 4 5 6 |
| 21. I'm overly sensitive to criticism. | 1 2 3 4 5 6 |
| 22. When my spouse or partner is away for too long, I feel like I am missing a part of me. | 1 2 3 4 5 6 |
| 23. I'm fairly self-accepting. | 1 2 3 4 5 6 |
| 24. I often feel that my spouse or partner wants too much from me. | 1 2 3 4 5 6 |
| 25. I try to live up to my parents' expectations. | 1 2 3 4 5 6 |
| 26. If I have had an argument with my spouse or partner, I tend to think about it all day. | 1 2 3 4 5 6 |
| 27. I am able to say no to others even when I feel pressured by them. | 1 2 3 4 5 6 |
| 28. When one of my relationships becomes very intense, I feel the urge to run away from it. | 1 2 3 4 5 6 |
| 29. Arguments with my parent(s) or sibling(s) can still make me feel awful. | 1 2 3 4 5 6 |
| 30. If someone is upset with me, I can't seem to let it go easily. | 1 2 3 4 5 6 |
| 31. I'm less concerned that others approve of me than I am about doing what I think is right. | 1 2 3 4 5 6 |
| 32. I would never consider turning to any of my family members for emotional support. | 1 2 3 4 5 6 |
| 33. I find myself thinking a lot about my relationship with my spouse or partner. | 1 2 3 4 5 6 |
| 34. I'm very sensitive to being hurt by others. | 1 2 3 4 5 6 |

| | |
|---|---|
| 35. My self-esteem really depends on how others think of me. | 1 2 3 4 (5) 6 |
| 36. When I'm with my spouse or partner, I often feel smothered | 1 2 (3) 4 5 6 |
| 37. I worry about people close to me getting sick, hurt, or upset. | 1 2 3 4 5 (6) |
| 38. I often wonder about the kind of impression I create. | 1 2 3 4 5 (6) |
| 39. When things go wrong, talking about them usually makes it worse. | (1) 2 3 4 5 6 |
| 40. I feel things more intensely than others do. | 1 2 3 4 5 (6) |
| 41. I usually do what I believe is right regardless of what others say. | 1 2 3 4 (5) 6 |
| 42. Our relationship might be better if my spouse or partner would give me the space I need. | 1 2 3 4 (5) 6 |
| 43. I tend to feel pretty stable under stress. | 1 2 3 (4) 5 6 |

Add up the scores (an underlined item means it is reversed; i.e., if you answer with a "6" to item 1, you'll need to re-key it as a 1 before averaging) accordingly for each subscale of the Differentiation of Self Inventory:

## EMOTIONAL REACTIVITY

1, 6, 10, 14, 18, 21, 26, 30, 34, 38, 40     *23*

*2 4 4 5 2 1 1 1 1 1 1*

Emotional reactivity happens because your intellect and emotions are fused together. You have difficulty remaining calm in response to the emotionality of others. You tend to make decisions based on what feels right. In other words, you're trapped in an emotional world. In a romantic relationship, emotional reactivity tends to happen in the codependent stage of the relationship. You're still fused together but trying to fight for separation, which leads to emotionally lashing out.

## EMOTIONAL CUTOFF

2, 3, 8, 12, 16, 20, 24, 28, 32, 36, 39, 42

Your personification is the reactive emotional distance. You appear aloof and isolated from others. You display an exaggerated face of independence. In turn, you may find intimacy profoundly threatening. You're either lashing out or you tend to shut down and emotionally cut your partner off in an attempt to create your own space. You have the need stay in the independent stage, which makes it difficult for you to build an intimate connection with your partner.

## FUSION WITH OTHERS

5, 9, 13, 17, 22, 25, 29, 33, 37

You're still highly fused and emotionally stuck in the role that you have occupied in your family of origin. You have a few firmly held convictions and beliefs that are your own. You are either dogmatic or compliant, and have tendencies to seek acceptance and approval from others above all other goals. This enmeshment tendency tends to create dependency in a relationship. Experience separation is overwhelming for you, which may be problematic as the relationship evolves.

## "I" POSITION

4, 7, 11, 15, 19, 23, 27, 31, 35, 41, 43

You have the ability to experience intimacy with and independence from others. You're able to maintain a clear, defined sense of self and thoughtfully adhere to personal convictions, even when being pressured by others to do otherwise. You allow for flexible boundaries when permitted emotional intimacy and physical union with another without a fear of merging or losing yourself. This occurs in the interdependent stage of a relationship.

When you're in the "I" position, you're differentiated, and are able to balance your emotions and intellect autonomously as well as intimately in a relationship. You're able to distinguish your thoughts from feelings and recognize what is guiding your choices. You're an independent thinker. You have your own emotions and take ownership of them. You recognize that you're a separate entity from your partner. You have emotional separation from your partner; you don't take on their emotions and make them yours. You have your own life, your own identity, and your partner has his in a relationship. All this is positive because when you're able to achieve this, then you're more likely to move into the *interdependent* or *rapprochement stage*.

It helped to have Terri fill her week with activities so she could focus on herself. But she is still anxious and worries about what Richard might do with his time. She also feels insignificant and unwanted because she feels if she were important enough to him, then he would have dropped what he needed to do to be with her. The struggle between those feelings and knowing intellectually what she needed to do was not easy. As I said, moving through the differentiation phase leaves one feeling very vulnerable and requires courage.

You would have thought it would be easier for Richard, as he's now free to do whatever he wants. He's got the "hall pass" or the "get-out-of-jail-free" card. But it wasn't. He felt guilty when he was out because he thought it was selfish of him. He was concerned about Terri's well-being; he wanted to take care of her feelings and make her happy. But he was also fully aware, after our discussion, that not going out will only feed into their unhealthy dynamic and enable her behavior. It may temporarily make her feel better, but it won't keep her happy in the long run.

For months, we continued to focus on the struggle between their hearts and heads, their feelings and logical thoughts, their emotions and behaviors. We explored more of their behaviors and their functions. We found out that Richard was the man of the house growing up. His father left when he was twelve years old. As an older child, he had to step up to help his mom take care of his younger siblings. Life wasn't easy, as she had to work two jobs to provide for him and his sisters. There were days he found his mom hiding in her room, crying. He did his best to help her in any way he was capable of. He comforted her when he could. He loves and admires her. She gave everything she had to raising him and his siblings. He knows that his mom had to be a very strong woman to do what she did. But when he sees her cry, he believes those are moments of weakness where she needs to be taken care of. He made a promise to himself that he would never be like his dad. He would never leave, and he would never make a woman cry. He doesn't want anyone to experience what his mom did.

We also looked into Terri's insecurity and her perception of self. She believes that she is not worthy of love. She goes through life with a set of beliefs that people will eventually abandon her. We also looked into her attachment styles and how they shaped who she is as a person.

As they came to understand why they do what they do, it was easier for them to change their behavior. They're also now more understanding of their partner's behavior. Terri has become less controlling; consequently, this helped Richard to feel less angry and resentful. Terri feels more worthy and lovable knowing Richard happily gives up his soccer games with the guys once in a while to be with her. She is more pleasant company to be around, which makes Richard *want* to spend more time with her, and when he's not with her, she is more understanding, which has alleviated a huge amount of guilt for him.

After many uphill battles, they've begun to see the freedom their changes have brought into their relationship by giving each other breathing room. They regain their sense of self with their own hobbies, interests, and direction in life. They're more in charge and in control of their own thoughts and feelings instead of depending on their partner to take care of them. They have each taken back the power and knowledge of how to make themselves happy. They realize their role and take ownership of their individuality within the duality of a two-person relationship. They operate as true partners, doing what they are good at in order to move more fluidly in this beautiful rhythm of a dance.

It was through this practicing phase that Terri learned what it means to trust. You can't have trust without giving someone an opportunity to earn it. Richard certainly got his opportunity, and passed with flying colors. **Trust is the cornerstone of every true love**. Terri faced her anxiety of the unknown and the uncontrollable. Each time she sits without reacting to her fear of not knowing what Richard is doing—if he is being faithful while he's out, if he is coming back to her—she allows him the opportunity to show her that he *does* indeed come back, that he *is* trustworthy. He is faithful, and best of all, when he says he'll call, he does it on the dot. The consistency of his words and actions gives her the sense of security, create stability, and reinforces the foundation of trust.

I can't tell you how excited I am to see them moving into this *rapprochement stage* of a relationship, where the couple is interdependent. They mutually love and respect one another. Despite countless afternoons when they would sit in my office blaming each other, pointing fingers at one another, raising their voices to ensure that they were being heard, and hoping that the other person understood, they have learned to recognize the role each plays in their relationship. They've learned to take ownership of their wrongdoing and to apologize when needed. There was crying and there was laughing; the dynamic was incredible with everything they brought into the therapy room. There was one key component they possessed that every successful relationship must have—knowing when, and when not, to quit. They didn't quit. They believed that their problems could be solved. I'm grateful that they trusted me enough when I told them in the beginning that whatever it was they were feeling, thinking, and dealing with, as long as they were willing to verbalize it, then we could work through it; and we have!

## What Does the Rapprochement Stage Look Like?

The answer to that question best comes from Terri:

"I didn't think this was possible. I always wanted to go back to the way we were. But it's even better than it was in the beginning. I'm so happy. We're able to honestly talk to each other about how we feel and what we want. We don't have to tiptoe around each other, afraid of hurting each other's feelings. We're able to take care of our own needs. I'm not dependent on him, feeling help-less when he fails to do what I had silently wished he would do. And I'm definitely not trying to change him anymore."

Richard hangs onto every word coming out of Terri's mouth. They're sitting next to each other, with her hand in his resting on her lap, Richard nodding periodically as she describes the dynamic of their new relationship.

When a couple is able to make it to this stage, they're able to have what we all want and hope for in a relationship: a strong, supportive, loving-dyad system. We feel that we're each other's first priority. We want to put our partner first, but not out of fear or trying to impress, and certainly not out of obligation. It's simply and purely because *we want to*. It is because we love our partner more than words can describe.

Better yet, you're not losing yourself doing it. You still have your strong individuality; you know who you are in the relationship. You're not forfeiting or sacrificing your needs for the other person. You're not afraid of intimacy or getting too close for fear of being suffocated or engulfed. You know the balance of ebbs and flows between intimacy and independence. You're able to negotiate and work together better as a result of having developed a clear sense of identity. You're nurturing and promoting the growth of each other. You want to see the relationship unfold, grow, change, and evolve as it needs to.

Time doesn't stand still. Life is not stagnant. Happiness is a moving target, and so is the depth of your relationship. You can't force a moth to stay in a cocoon forever. It will die. Like a butterfly going through metamorphosis, you must allow your relationship to evolve, to transform. When you're balancing the "me," "we," and "you," it will help you reach your relationship goals without losing sight of your individual dream or destroying your partner's.

Successful coupling is not just a dream. It is a reality. But for any dream to come true, you have to work hard at it.

## WHICH STAGE OF A RELATIONSHIP ARE YOU IN?

Terri and Richard were moving into rapprochement together. However, not every couple can move at the same pace. Recognizing the stage that you and your partner are in can help you set the pace as well as see each other's needs. When you know each other's needs, you'll be able to work better together to reach your ultimate goal.

Like Terri and Richard did, many couples thank me for the success of their relationship. But the truth is, they did most of the hard work. It was their time, effort, and investment that they were willing to make for themselves, for each other, and for their relationship that made it work. That's what makes love beautiful—what we're willing to do to have true love and keep our relationships alive.

## [ 4 ]

# *Our First Love*

> Being deeply loved by someone gives you
> strength, while loving someone deeply gives
> you courage.
>
> —Lao Tzu

WE ALL WANT true love, and our success in having the love of our lives has a lot to do with our first love. I'm not talking about your puppy love or the first girlfriend or boyfriend you had, or even the first serious one you brought home to introduce to your parents. As a matter of fact, your first true love is your parents— your primary caregivers when you were an infant.

Most of us don't think about how our attachment to our parents is related to our approaches in dating. Nine out of ten times, when I have clients who have fears of commitment or abandonment, they say something along the lines of: "My mom lost me at the market," "My mom passed away when I was young," "My dad forgot to pick me up from school," "My dad's not in the picture anymore," "My parents got a divorce," "My boyfriend broke up with me," "My girlfriend cheated on me," and so on. It is usually such life events or circumstances they consciously remember that they believe led to the fear of abandonment they feel today. But those events only further reinforce the embedded fear of abandonment when their needs weren't met at an early age.

Fear of abandonment is at the heart of commitment issues. People who have a fear of commitment are ultimately afraid of giving themselves to another person, subsequently being vulnerable at the possibility of being abandoned or rejected.

We tend to remember the pain that left us with nasty scars, so it makes sense that we would want to avoid re-experiencing that pain. That's what is keeping us from going into a relationship or being open to a new one. But how many of us can honestly say we remember what happened to us from the day we were born up until one year of age or so? Chances are, not many of us, if any. Our approach to adult relationships is shaped not only by conscious pains but also unconscious fires. The good news is, we can still figure out the unconscious events that occurred in our lives even before we were two years old. Our attachment styles to our primary caregivers create love links. It is essentially our love personality which affects our relationships—particularly romantic ones—later in life. When your first true love was in love with you and treated you accordingly, then you'll go through life believing that you're worthy of love and lovable. Otherwise, you'll have a different perception of yourself.

## The Four Stages of Attachment

The crucial foundation of attachment forms before we are even two years old. There are four stages of attachment: The *preattachment stage* occurs from birth to three months. Some parents realize that in the first three months of its life, the baby doesn't care about them. In this stage, infants don't show attachment to any specific caregiver. The natural crying and fussing is a call for any caregiver to attend to its needs. The baby's positive response (for example, the baby stops crying after being fed) encourages the caregiver to remain close by. But some infants are more temperamental than others and more difficult to soothe. This can create frustration and feelings of defeat in new parents, which can lead to harmful, resigned behavior that will affect the child in the long run.

The second stage is *indiscriminate attachment,* which happens around six weeks to seven months. In this stage, infants begin to show preferences for primary and secondary caregivers and begin to develop *trust* that the caregivers will respond to their needs. This trust is crucial in the development of intimacy and whether a person feels worthy of love in future relationships. Additionally, babies are able to distinguish between familiar and unfamiliar faces as they approach seven months old.

In the *discriminate attachment stage,* which is about seven to eleven months old, the infant shows strong preferences and forms attachment to one specific caregiver. Infants will show distress when separated from a primary attachment figure, which is referred to as *separation anxiety.* Also, infants will have anxiety around strangers.

Lastly, the *multiple attachment stage* occurs approximately after nine months. During this stage, infants form strong bonds and attachment with others beyond the primary caregiver, such as the other parent, siblings, and relatives.

Through these stages of attachment, depending on the response of the primary caregiver, four types of attachment styles can develop. The quality of caregiving—how sensitive the parents are to their baby's signals—determines the development of a particular attachment style during this critical period. When caregivers respond quickly and consistently, children learn that they're "good enough." They can depend on the people who are responsible for taking care of their needs.

When children believe they can trust or count on their caregivers to be dependable and reliable, it gives them a sense of security. When in need or frightened, they will seek out their attachment figure because they know their needs will be met. They know they will be comforted and reassured. This sense of security also gives children the confidence to explore their environment. They know they can go back to their secure base of their attachment figure when they're in distress. They will carry this feeling of security with them and feel this way the rest of their lives. They know they have a secure base and can freely come and go without fear; this creates a secure form of attachment. As mentioned earlier, securely attached children show stress when separated from their caregiver; however, they're secure enough to feel assured that the caregiver will return.

This early, secure attachment style with the primary caregiver will lead to secure attachment in adulthood which I refer to as a **Keeper**. You're ready to love and receive love. As a securely attached individual, you'll be open and able to create meaningful relationships. You believe and trust that you're good enough to have your needs met, which enables you to seek support from your partner. You'll also be more emotionally in tune and empathetic to both yours and your partner's needs, and will be able to set healthy boundaries while maintaining your personal space. You also won't have anxiety when you're apart from your partner for fear your partner won't come back or abandon you. However, if you have an *ambivalent attachment style,* that would be one of your greatest fears.

## How Do You End Up with an Ambivalent Attachment Style?

An *ambivalent attachment style* is characterized by anxious behavior. It happens when the attachment figure was inconsistent in responding to your needs as an infant. Sometimes your needs were met, and sometimes they were not. You couldn't depend on the caregiver to be there when you were in need. This inconsistent behavior leads us to exhibit clingy and dependent behavior as children and adults. We become very distressed when the attachment figure leaves, due to our doubting their return, and we don't have the confidence to explore novel experiences due to our fear of not knowing if our caregiver will be there when we come back.

When in distress, children with ambivalent attachment are very difficult to soothe. They do not feel comforted by their interactions with the attachment figure. They stay angry. This behavior later shows in their adult relationship with their significant other, who is a new attachment figure. If you are in a relationship with a partner with this type of attachment, it can be difficult to soothe your partner when in distress. It is necessary to provide a safe space for such people so that they can learn to soothe themselves. However, it is essential that you let the person know you're available when needed. Make sure that you're there; otherwise, you further reinforce this fear.

This insecure ambivalence from childhood results in anxious and insecure attachment in adulthood, which I call a **Chaser**. They chase the good feelings of being wanted and desired.

People with this attachment style want to form intimacy and tend to chase after it. Chasers also have a great fear of abandonment for not being "good enough." These individuals tend to be clingy and controlling; they also exhibit erratic and unpredictable behavior that can push people away. However, they also can be very sweet and charming, traits they have developed to attract others in order to get more favorable responses, which can lead to forming attachments. In other words, they believe they are less deserving of love and must work hard to earn love and affection.

Do you remember Terri and Richard? Teri's insecurity and clingy behavior is an example of a Chaser as a result of insecure ambivalent attachment in her childhood. She was anxious and controlling of Richard's activities. As a child, she was not able to do that with her attachment figures, but as an adult, she tries to curb the behavior of others in an attempt to alleviate her own anxiety and prevent others from leaving her. Terri has strong needs and desires to maintain closeness and the physical presence of her significant other. It's problematic when Richard leaves or when he is not with her, as she is uncertain whether he will come back. She can't fathom the idea that he could behave consistently toward her. This creates a tremendous fear in her that he won't be available to her when she needs him, just like her caregiver wasn't available.

In addition to her fear of abandonment, Terri also had this nearly debilitating fear of rejection by her partner. Children with ambivalent attachment, or Chasers, tend to have a negative self-image due to the inconsistent and unpredictable behavior of their caregiver. Each time a caregiver failed to be there, it was a form of rejection. When your supposed first love (the one who chose to bring you into this world) was not in love with you unconditionally and failed to consistently care for you, then it's easy to believe that nothing is going to stop your current partner from doing the same thing.

## How Do You End Up with an Avoidant Attachment Style?

When you have ambivalent attachment, you've had the experience of knowing how it feels to have your needs met, albeit not all the time. When your needs were being met, it felt great. It made you feel validated and worthwhile, as you were loved. You cling to that and put yourself out there, time and time again, working really hard and doing whatever you can to get that positive reinforcement, even if it means facing the fear of real or perceived rejection and abandonment.

Sadly, children with *avoidant attachment* styles don't feel the same. Children of avoidance attachment grow up to be avoidant of intimacy as adults. I call them **Runners**.

It is understandable; children with avoidant attachment had parents who were unreliable, insensitive, unavailable, and outright rejecting of their children's needs. In a worst-case scenario, their parents might also have been neglectful. Therefore, when they are in a relationship that starts to get close, their fear and mistrust resurface, and they need to distance themselves.

Children with avoidant attachment style unconsciously believe that their needs will not be met. They're not "good enough" to be cared for. Hence, they will not rely on or seek help from a caregiver when in distress. These children become independent of their attachment figure, emotionally and physically. When offered choices, they show no preference between a caregiver and a complete stranger. These children grow up to be more rigid, critical, and intolerant. Runners tend to avoid closeness or emotional connections with others. It does not necessarily mean that deep down they don't want to have close, intimate relationships, but because they experienced rejection from a primary caregiver at an early age, they end up seeing themselves as full of flaws, unacceptable, and unlovable. However, because they yearn to be understood and loved, they work really hard to be very considerate and helpful at times in interpersonal relationships. They sometimes become people-pleasers, which is a behavior that may backfire as they eventually feel taken advantage of. This then leads them to feel more motivated to keep people out for fear of being used or hurt.

There is a second subset of avoidance, which is the dismissive-avoidant. Dismissive-avoidants, or simply **Dismissers**, perhaps have experienced enough letdowns that they build up a fortress of defense mechanisms to keep people out. They will try to convince themselves and others to believe that they do not need to have close relationships with people.

*Christy*

Christy, who you met in Chapter 2 and who loves to fall in love quickly, exemplifies the Runner. She set out to find a man who's not like her father, who she believed had abandoned her. Christy's track record for relationships has been about three months. That's the longest, and the shortest is a week. She loves the attention and affection she initially receives, but soon after, she finds ways to sabotage the relationship. She finds ways to push her suitors away, cheat on them, or outright break up with them because she is no longer interested. She is insightful enough to know that she has that tendency, but just doesn't know how to stop it. Before helping Christy stop her sabotaging tendency, I needed to help her to understand why she does it in the first place.

"How does the cheating happen? Is it because the attention and affection stop?" I asked for clarification.

"Not always. Sometimes, it does, but most of the time it is still the same, if not more so."

"I see."

She quickly added, "Maybe because I think all men are like my father, who cheated on my mom. That's why they got divorced. So, I cheat on them first."

"So, you try to beat them to the punch. Better to do the rejecting than being rejected. It gives you some sense of control, knowing what's going to happen."

"Yes! But I hate myself for hurting them, though."

I know her father's situation exacerbates her defense mechanism, but it's not the cause.

"I know you said you want a man who is different from your father. You want someone who's attentive, understanding, and accepting of you. I'm curious; do you feel that you deserve it?"

She took some time to ponder the question. "No. It sounds weird, but no," she finally replied.

"Why not?"

"Because I suck."

"How so?"

"I'm depressed. I'm not interesting. I'm a cheater. I'm a terrible person who's going to hurt them ..."

I stopped her, as I'm certain she could continue on with the list of negative self-perceptions. "You don't sound too kind to yourself. You want to be accepted with unconditional regard, but when it's given to you by the men you date, you don't think you deserve it or believe it."

"How can that be true? My father couldn't accept me conditionally even when I was perfect. I got all A's in school, I danced, I played basketball, I was a cheerleader. I never got into trouble, I did whatever he asked, and nothing! As for my mother, well, I think she was very conditional with me. I think she has bipolar.

She was very hot and cold. Sometimes, she is really good, but when I got a C, not for the whole class, but for an assignment, she would make me feel horrible."

From what Christy is describing, it's fair to say that her father was absent, and her mother was inconsistent at best and unavailable at worst. She allows herself to engage in romantic interactions with men, but only on a very surface level, when it's still superficial. She doesn't allow herself to have a deep emotional connection with any of them. She doesn't trust their intentions. She doesn't believe that they would stay once they discovered her flaws and who she is as a person. She believes she has to be perfect to have love.

It is important for me to point out that how she sees herself is distorted, but that doesn't stop her from sabotaging herself. That's her defense mechanism—an unhealthy one, but one nevertheless. It helps her to remain distant from others, and that is the safest place to be. No one can hurt her if she doesn't allow them in.

*Eliot*

Eliot is thirty-three-year-old man who never had a serious relationship as an adult. His sister encouraged him to seek help. He never thought he needed therapy and still shows reservations, but he's willing to give it a try, even though he doesn't think it's any better than a sounding board. He admits that it's hard to find a woman he's really interested in. They come few and far between, and oftentimes if he is interested in them, he doesn't approach them. A normal person would rule out confidence issues. Why would a young, successful doctor have this problem? He's fit, six feet tall, dark hair, blue eyes, funny, and generally pretty easy to talk to—but confidence comes in all shapes and sizes. I asked him what his reasons were for not approaching the ladies.

"Sometimes, it's not at the right time or place ..." He let the words hang on his tongue.

"And others ...?" I asked.

"Guts. Having the balls to do it."

I have come to find out that there are only a few women he finds interesting, but he's only interested from afar, like looking at a mirage. He doesn't approach them, and that's the reason why he finds them interesting. As soon as he approaches them, he quickly loses his interest. He is still open to dating, but for him, dating is to pass the time while waiting for the right one to come along. Generally, he doesn't open himself up emotionally, but when he finds himself able to do so, she doesn't stimulate either of his heads. The women he has chemistry with and can have an intellectually stimulating conversation with, he can't open up to emotionally. A couple of women he found himself attracted to, respected intellectually, and could open up emotionally to happened to be married or in a serious relationship. Eliot believed that all of the good ones were taken, or he just hasn't found the right one, while his friends think that he's just too picky. He is another classic example of a Runner.

Like Christy, Eliot exhibits this great sense of autonomy, since this has been his practice from an early age. People like Christy and Eliot who are Runners focus on things that they believe are within their control, such as school, career, and hobbies. Their autonomy is hiding behind walls of insecurities, fears, and disappointments. They believe what they want is not going to happen, so there's no point of trying or opening themselves up for love. While they may have a romanticized image of love, they're more skeptical and cynical in their approach to it. They believe that their needs are not going to be met, just like when they were young. Sometimes consciously, but often unconsciously, they don't allow themselves to be available emotionally. They don't let

to be in a relationship with someone who has a disorganized attachment style. Sometimes, you feel that you can change people with this attachment style or help them change. But it's not something you can really help them with, because they need to do some serious soul searching and introspection; they need to understand themselves and the roots of their behavior and must make the active decision to change themselves along with professional help.

## CAN YOU CHANGE YOUR ATTACHMENT STYLE?

Attachment styles are unconscious formations that you have very little control over, since they formed when you were young. Since you were an infant, you don't remember how your primary caregiver responded to you. You can't go back and change the bond of attachment you had with your primary caregiver. However, you do have control of your attachment style today, and you can change it. I'd like you to take a look at your relationships today and identify which of these attachment styles you are most aligned with. Or, to make it easier for you, take the next five minutes to complete the Experiences in Close Relationships/Revised Adult Attachment questionnaire below to find out which category you currently belong to.

**Directions**: The statements below concern how you feel in emotionally intimate relationships. We are interested in how you generally experience relationships, not just in what is happening in a current relationship. Respond to each statement by circling a number to indicate how much you agree or disagree with the statement. A score of "1" means you strongly disagree; a score of "7" means you strongly agree.

| 1 | I rarely worry about my partner leaving me. | 1 | 2 | 3 | 4 | 5 | 6 | 7 |
|---|---|---|---|---|---|---|---|---|
| 2 | I find it easy to depend on romantic partners. | 1 | 2 | 3 | 4 | 5 | 6 | 7 |
| 3 | I talk things over with my partner. | 1 | 2 | 3 | 4 | 5 | 6 | 7 |
| 4 | When I show my feelings for romantic partners, I'm afraid they will not feel the same about me. | 1 | 2 | 3 | 4 | 5 | 6 | 7 |
| 5 | My partner only seems to notice me when I'm angry. | 1 | 2 | 3 | 4 | 5 | 6 | 7 |
| 6 | I often worry that my partner will not want to stay with me. | 1 | 2 | 3 | 4 | 5 | 6 | 7 |
| 7 | I don't feel comfortable opening up to romantic partners. | 1 | 2 | 3 | 4 | 5 | 6 | 7 |
| 8 | I worry a lot about my relationships. | 1 | 2 | 3 | 4 | 5 | 6 | 7 |
| 9 | It helps to turn to my romantic partner in times of need. | 1 | 2 | 3 | 4 | 5 | 6 | 7 |
| 10 | My desire to be very close sometimes scares people away. | 1 | 2 | 3 | 4 | 5 | 6 | 7 |
| 11 | I'm afraid that I will lose my partner's love. | 1 | 2 | 3 | 4 | 5 | 6 | 7 |
| 12 | I tell my partner just about everything. | 1 | 2 | 3 | 4 | 5 | 6 | 7 |
| 13 | It makes me mad that I don't get the affection and support I need from my partner. | 1 | 2 | 3 | 4 | 5 | 6 | 7 |
| 14 | Sometimes romantic partners change their feelings about me for no apparent reason. | 1 | 2 | 3 | 4 | 5 | 6 | 7 |

| 15 | I usually discuss my problems and concerns with my partner. | 1 | 2 | 3 | 4 | 5 | 6 | 7 |
|----|----|----|----|----|----|----|----|----|
| 16 | My romantic partner makes me doubt myself. | 1 | 2 | 3 | 4 | 5 | 6 | 7 |
| 17 | I am very comfortable being close to romantic partners. | 1 | 2 | 3 | 4 | 5 | 6 | 7 |
| 18 | I prefer not to be too close to romantic partners. | 1 | 2 | 3 | 4 | 5 | 6 | 7 |
| 19 | I feel comfortable depending on romantic partners. | 1 | 2 | 3 | 4 | 5 | 6 | 7 |
| 20 | I feel comfortable sharing my private thoughts and feelings with my partner. | 1 | 2 | 3 | 4 | 5 | 6 | 7 |
| 21 | My partner really understands me and my needs. | 1 | 2 | 3 | 4 | 5 | 6 | 7 |
| 22 | It's not difficult for me to get close to my partner. | 1 | 2 | 3 | 4 | 5 | 6 | 7 |
| 23 | I prefer not to show a partner how I feel deep down. | 1 | 2 | 3 | 4 | 5 | 6 | 7 |
| 24 | When my partner is out of sight, I worry that he or she might become interested in someone else. | 1 | 2 | 3 | 4 | 5 | 6 | 7 |
| 25 | I find that my partner(s) don't want to get as close as I would like. | 1 | 2 | 3 | 4 | 5 | 6 | 7 |
| 26 | I often worry that my partner doesn't really love me. | 1 | 2 | 3 | 4 | 5 | 6 | 7 |
| 27 | I worry that romantic partners won't care about me as much as I care about them. | 1 | 2 | 3 | 4 | 5 | 6 | 7 |
| 28 | I am nervous when partners get too close to me. | 1 | 2 | 3 | 4 | 5 | 6 | 7 |

| 29 | I find it relatively easy to get close to my partner. | 1 | 2 | 3 | 4 | 5 | 6 | 7 |
|----|----|---|---|---|---|---|---|---|
| 30 | I get uncomfortable when a romantic partner wants to be very close. | 1 | 2 | 3 | 4 | 5 | 6 | 7 |
| 31 | I often wish that my partner's feelings for me were as strong as my feelings for him or her. | 1 | 2 | 3 | 4 | 5 | 6 | 7 |
| 32 | I do not often worry about being abandoned. | 1 | 2 | 3 | 4 | 5 | 6 | 7 |
| 33 | I worry that I won't measure up to other people. | 1 | 2 | 3 | 4 | 5 | 6 | 7 |
| 34 | I'm afraid that once a romantic partner gets to know me, he or she won't like who I really am. | 1 | 2 | 3 | 4 | 5 | 6 | 7 |
| 35 | It's easy for me to be affectionate with my partner. | 1 | 2 | 3 | 4 | 5 | 6 | 7 |
| 36 | I find it difficult to allow myself to depend on romantic partners. | 1 | 2 | 3 | 4 | 5 | 6 | 7 |

To obtain your score, you need to add up your responses. (Underlined means reversed scored, i.e., if you answer with a "6" to item 1, you'll need to re-key it as a 2 before averaging. You'll need to reverse the answers to those questions before averaging the responses).

## ATTACHMENT-RELATED ANXIETY:
1, 4, 5, 6, 8, 10, 11, 13, 14, 16, 24, 25, 26, 27, 31, 32, 33, 34

## ATTACHMENT-RELATED AVOIDANCE:
2, 3, 7, 9, 12, 15, 17, 18, 19, 20, 21, 22, 23, 28, 29, 30, 35, 36

When you recognize the pattern of your attachment style, you can get to the bottom of your fear and insecurity. All fear must be faced before it can be conquered. When you know your fear, then you're able to see the defense mechanism that you have developed over the years, and thus you can change it. The good news is that about sixty percent of the population has a secure attachment style. Statistically speaking, that means you have a great chance of meeting someone who is securely attached and will be able to help you get your needs met. But you must be able to recognize them and not push them away. They can and will love you and won't abandon you. You don't have to let the fear of your past dictate your future. I hope you have the courage and allow yourself to open up to love and to be loved. That's the only way that you can have the love of your life—your soulmate.

# 5

# The Blessings
# and a Curse

We waste time looking for the perfect lover,
instead of creating the perfect love.

—Tom Robbins

UNFORTUNATELY, NOT ALL of us had an upbringing that
was nurturing and fostered a secure attachment. We end up going through life holding onto our inner child's wound, believing
that's how love is. This is a treacherous curse that, sadly, some of
us suffer—but we don't have to endure it for the rest of our lives.

Rather than simply blame our parents, we can look at this as
an opportunity to recognize our issues and correct the problem
of our perception towards love and affection. There are many ex-
plainable reasons why some parents do not meet their children's

needs. It could be negligence, lack of education and knowledge in the psychology of healthy parenting, or simply life circumstances. In instances when a child's needs are not immediately or consistently met, it can lead to the unconscious belief that their needs are not important or they have to work really hard in order for their needs to be met.

One of the popular beliefs I have heard is that you have to let your child learn to self-soothe when they're crying. As an infant, generally speaking, if the child's needs were met, they wouldn't be crying for your attention. If children are successfully able to learn to self-soothe, they internalize the belief that they are insignificant and their needs will not be met by others. This belief unfortunately leads to avoidance attachment tendencies growing up.

Using the two scores gained from the questionnaires in the previous chapters, you can identify your attachment style as an adult. Securely attached is represented as the "low" end of both scores; in other words, a secure individual does not worry about whether their partner will abandon them (low anxiety) and is comfortable opening up to and depending on others (low avoidance). The insecure end would be high anxiety and high avoidance. By combining the two-dimensional scores, you'll be able to identify your exact attachment style using the diagram below.

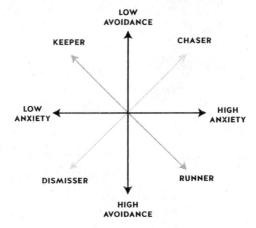

You may have heard that "opposites attract" or "you attract people who are the same as you." Both are correct; you do attract people who are similar to you, as well as completely different from you, depending on your attachment style. Keepers who are securely attached tend to attract other secure individuals. Having been brought up with responsive caregivers, secure individuals feel safe in relying on others for comfort and care and are able to provide love and affection in return. When two Keepers meet, they're able to be open and honest in expressing their feelings without fear of rejection, and there is no doubt that love is real, mutual, and tangible. Secures, or Keepers, are more successful at getting into a relationship and maintaining a happy one, which makes them less available in the dating pool at a later age.

Keepers do cross paths with other types of attachment; unfortunately, the chemistry is often absent and no spark is seen. When there is an inner child's wound, we unconsciously attract the people who feel right but who are very wrong for us. We attract and get attached to people who help us feel better on the conscious level, which only further reinforces our unconscious fears and wounds. There is a seemingly unexplainable chemistry (or lack thereof), even when you find someone objectively attractive. Chemistry ignites from the unconscious wounds. As Carl Jung once said, "Until you make the unconscious conscious, it will direct your life and you will call it fate."

## HOW DO OTHER ATTACHMENTS ATTRACT?

Dismissers tend to avoid attachment and intimacy due to a faulty belief that needing others is a weakness and that attachment is a string that ties you down. Hence, Dismissers tend to isolate themselves and create pseudo-independency by focusing on themselves, and may be overly attending to their habits and comforts. Dismissers are rarely open about declaring themselves, which can create an irresistible mystery when it comes to dating. They can also be very charming and socially gracious; however, don't count on them to pursue a real intimate relationship. If a Dismisser is in a relationship, there is very little, if any, emotional connection and commitment. When a Dismisser feels attachment, they will sabotage the relationship by pushing their partner away. In heated or emotional situations, the Dismisser will shut down emotionally and keep you out. They stay true to their dismissive tendency and attitude of not caring whether you stay or go.

Runners share the fear that deep down, they're not worthy of love and are distrusting of others, like the Dismissers, but haven't completely given up on love and intimacy. Runners struggle with the yearning for intimacy, yet are afraid of being too close. They try to keep their emotions in check and at bay, particularly when it comes to their object of affection. Runners typically will not pursue a relationship with someone they see the potential for a real future with. The person that they want to go for is the same person they are afraid of getting close to for fear of rejection and abandonment. They end up having temporary quasi-intimacy with people who they feel safe with and have no fear of letting go, as real love and attachment were never formed.

Chasers have heightened anxiety and fear of abandonment fueled by insatiate emotional hunger for intimacy. Chasers are desperate to form closeness and an attachment bond. They have a fantasy connection, or rather an illusion, that attachment can complete them, hence they would relentlessly pursue and do anything to earn that love and affection. Chasers falsely believe that they have to constantly prove themselves and work hard to earn love. When love is freely given, they will not believe it, since they haven't earned it. In a relationship, they often are clingy, demanding, and possessive, particularly when feeling insecure or doubtful of their partner. To their demise, they exacerbate their own fear of being abandoned when their partner needs space or is simply just being independent.

You still have a chance at having true love, even when you don't have secure attachment from birth. However, you must recognize and acknowledge your attachment style and your approach to love. It is important to keep in mind that when you're anxious, fearful, and dismissive, you tend to attract similar people. This is due to your unconscious wounds.

Dismissers and Runners rarely get together, since they both are avoidants. They will avoid approaching one another. If they do approach each other, it's not for the long haul, because both are non-committal and fearful of intimacy. A relationship with either type can seem easy and non-demanding in the beginning; however, when conflicts arise, they will be swept under the rug instead of worked through. Without prevarication, it's much easier to walk away, since no real intimacy was formed. Two Chaser individuals in a relationship with each other will be overly zealous in the beginning, which can be overwhelming, and when it comes to conflicts, they will fight (to their detriment) and eventually become too suffocating to handle.

A dangerous combination is when you have a Chaser coupling with a Runner or a Dismisser. These two tend to attract one another based on what I call empathetic love. It's empathy of the unconscious wound—fear of abandonment for not being good enough. When we feel that we're not good enough, we yearn to be accepted by others. The Chaser's strong need for attachment creates their persistent pursuing tendencies, whereas an avoidant's natural tendency is to create distance (even though they may be entertaining the idea of intimacy from the pursuit). This creates a cyclical approach-avoidance dynamic in the relationship. The unfortunate part is that the Chaser often doesn't see it that way and will try even harder. We all make mistakes, even when it comes to love, but we need to learn from our mistakes and not let history repeat itself. If it doesn't work out the second time, it won't happen the third time. When it happens the second time, it's no longer a mistake—it's a choice.

Whether you're a Chaser, Runner, Dismisser, or Disrupter, you need to step out of your comfort zone and make a conscious change to gain the love of your life. You may attract one another or end up with a Keeper who is secured, but if you don't change your ways, it won't work. Choose to understand yourself and your partner. Choose to work together. Choose love. It's within each of us. We're capable of forming intimate relationships. Sometimes, we just need to change our ways to achieve it.

It's easy to categorize our attachment styles. However, when it comes to our personality, it can't neatly fit into a category. It's a spectrum of security or lack thereof and where on that spectrum that we fall on. On the next pages is a chart of more characteristics and behaviors of each attachment style.

| | CHARACTERISTICS |
|---|---|
| **KEEPER**<br>(Secure) | Securely attached • Confident • Empathetic • Effective communicator • Great listener • Consistent • Observant of other's feelings • Doesn't fear rejection • Doesn't let rejection negatively affect their sense of self • Knows one's selfworth • Loves unconditionally • Doesn't hold a grudge • Straightforward • Comfortable with intimacy • Mentally flexible • Emotionally available • Doesn't separate sex and love • Content • Can be comfortable and complacent at times • Takes each other's words at face value |
| **CHASER**<br>(Anxious) | Craves intimacy and closeness • Doubtful of one's self-worth • Can be "needy" and "clingy" • Has the need to prove oneself • Can be very sociable • Constant need for attention and reassurance • Doesn't feel "good enough" • Strong will • Feels things deeply • Emotionally reactive • Critical of self and partner • Cares more about partner and what they think • Tends to be manipulative • Controlling • Needs other's approval • Black or white mentality • Fear of being abandoned • Very giving and generous • Pursuer in life and love • Fierce • Likeable and charming • A giver and people pleaser • Persistent |
| **RUNNER**<br>(Fearful-Avoidant) | Distrusting of others • Needs to be in control • Confident • Wants intimacy but is fearful of it • Guarded • Fear of rejection • Has difficulty with feelings and emotions • Logical • Dislikes introspection • Doesn't feel deserving of love and affection • Highly critical • Aloof • Tends to cut people off and out of their life • Exhibits a likeable persona to gain other's approval • Emotionally unavailable • Tends to be sensitive and gets hurt easily • Needs to be needed • Sensitive to criticism • Tends to be generous but emotionally stingy • Doesn't feel deserving of love • Inconsistent • Unrealistic expectations of partner |
| **DISMISSER**<br>(Dismissive-Avoidant) | Values self-sufficiency and independence • Charming and socially gracious • Highly guarded • Fearful of looking inward • Tends to have the "I'm good and I don't need others" mentality • Tends to believe needing others is weak • Highly sensitive • Extremely critical of others • Doesn't have a very trusting world view • Has superficial self-esteem • Has strong traits of narcissism • Doesn't feel worthy of love at the core • Emotionally unavailable or stingy • Terrified of getting rejected • Romanticize or idealize relationship • Dismissive tendencies • Can be very driven for social status and prestige • Hyper focused on petty flaws • Exaggerated sense of self importance |
| **DISRUPTER**<br>(Disorganized) | Disorganized in attachment and behavior. • Hot and cold tendencies • Charming and loving as well as hostile and abusive • Blaming habits • Highly insecure • Controlling and manipulative • Denial of personal flaws • Lack of personal responsibility or accountability • Send mixed messages • Lack of communication skills • Lack of emotional intelligence • Emotionally reactive • Has a need for significant sense of self-importance • Demand respect • Inconsistent • Accusatory habit • Destructive tendencies • Insincere repentant • Distrustful |

| | BEHAVIOR IN DATING AND RELATIONSHIP |
|---|---|
| **KEEPER** (Secure) | Genuinely honest with one's feelings and actions • Expresses interest when they are interested • Allows you to comfort and care for them • Attentive and responsive in caring for partner's needs and feelings • Expressive of inner thoughts and feelings • Does not withhold love and affection • Does not manipulate to get what they want • Openly and effectively communicates what they want and need • Does not keep you from knowing them for fear of rejection • They want to be known and understood • Will share their world with you (family, friends, work etc.) • Makes an effort to understand your point of view in conflicts • Works to come to solution that satisfied you both • Is not defensive nor has the need to punish or injure partner during a fight • Willing to examine one's ways and beliefs and make changes when necessary • Quick to forgive without holding onto anger and resentment • Treats you with love and respect |
| **CHASER** (Anxious) | Tends to try too hard to put best foot forward in the beginning • Tends to be a pursuer • Dives into relationship head first • Falls hard and fast in love • Too focused on one's effort that may miss subtle cues from partner at times • Doesn't give up • Has difficulty discussing feelings and needs honestly • Doesn't want to be alone when in a relationship • Gets anxious and preoccupied with the relationship • Constantly thinking about partner and the relationship • Tends to force intimacy or the relationship to happen • Tends to only remember good memories and qualities • Tends to put partner on the pedestal • Idealizes • Emotionally volatile and remorseful • Needs to be in constant contact with partner • Bitter when wants and needs are not being reciprocated • Believes "s/he's it" or "this is it" your only chance at love • Can be very tolerating of partner's negative behavior • Works hard to earn love and affection • Believes that partner can change and try to be the person to change partner • Tends to keep score or "tally up" • Has difficulty letting go or unhealthily holds on to relationship • Idealizes and devalues • Exhibits love/hate or hot/cold • Emotionally hostile when conflicts arise • Does things to make partner feel jealous • Manipulation • Pulling and pushing tendencies |
| **RUNNER** (Fearful-Avoidant) | Tends to be shy • Rarely takes initiative or puts oneself out there when it comes to dating • Tends to wait to be approached • Can be charming in courtship • Knows what is expected and follows dating protocol • Wants to form intimacy but pushes partner away when it happens • Tends to be in one's own head • Doesn't open up about one's wants, needs, thoughts and feelings • Focuses more on what's within one's control (i.e work) rather than the relationship • Not very invested in partner or relationship as it's not a top priority • Has unrealistic expectations for partner and relationship to fulfill • Allows partner's shortcomings and flaws to outweigh the goods • Fearful of getting too attached • Tends to create or manipulate situations for partner to be there for them without showing they need them • Cycling of emotionally closeness and distance • Receptive to connection when being initiated but creates distance when intimacy starts to form • Tries to create and maintain a distance from partner • Tends to wait for partner to initiate intimacy • Tries to use logic for emotional issues • Exhibits warm/cold tendencies or mixed messages • Threats to leave when feeling hurt or insecure • Needs partner to pursue or show grand gestures • Emotionally withdraws when conflicts arise |

| | BEHAVIOR IN DATING AND RELATIONSHIP |
|---|---|
| **DISMISSER** (Dismissive-Avoidant) | Plays well in the role of courtship • Has extreme difficulty with commitment (i.e. "I'm not ready to commit" but will stay together) • Afraid or almost incapable of tolerating true intimacy • Instinctively runs away when someone gets too close • Focuses on partner's small shortcomings or imperfections (i.e. the ways one dresses, walk, sit, etc.) • Tends to put the blame on partner • Pulls away when things are going well • Verbally or behaviorally lets partner know that they're low on the priority list • Un-empathic of partner's feelings and emotional needs • Creates distance or distances from partner • Forms relationship with emotionally unavailable individual (i.e. married) • Always avoids one or more forms of closeness or intimacy • Tends to mentally "check out" when partner talks • Maintains a distance from partner • Does not open up to partner • Tends to keep secrets or leave things "foggy" • Almost incapable of expressing feelings |
| **DISRUPTER** (Disorganized) | Can be very charming • Easily get jealous • Controlling of partner • Tend to put partner down • Hypersensitive to any criticism • Narcissistic • Have the victimization tendencies • Blame partner for anger outbursts • Tend to cut partner from social support network • Convince partner that all they need is each other • Apologetic and but not remorseful • Moody and unpredictable • Do use threats and force to intimidate partner • Blame others for their feelings and behavior • May try to create a superior-inferior relationship with partner • Can be intentionally cruel or hurtful • May think it's okay to resolve conflicts with violence • Secretive • Is not completely honest with partner • May want partner's idolization |

Consciously changing your behavior to create healthy attachment may seem unnatural. However, with practice, it will become easier and more natural. Also, you're not changing who you are as a person fundamentally. You are actually getting in touch with who you are at your core.

## WHAT ARE THE BLESSINGS?

My parents have been married over fifty years. They have been through more than one can fathom in a lifetime. They went through the Vietnam War, where the fall of one regime saw my dad in a re-education camp (communist jail) for more than seven years. My mother raised the children by herself while taking care of her parents and parents in-law. My parents met through an arranged marriage. They chose to obey their parents and followed tradition. Perhaps they didn't choose each other as lovers, but they chose to honor the blessings each day once they're committed to one another. They're as happily married, if not more so, than the day they were betrothed.

When you hear the word blessings, you probably think of God's favor or protection. But a blessing is not reserved only for a religious ceremony; a blessing is the belief that there is more to your relationship than just the two of you. My parents honor their parents' blessings. Blessings are an additional entity that helps strengthen your relationship as "a cord of three strands is not quickly broken."

It is important to talk about these blessings or protections, because when you have a protection, you're less vulnerable to its calamity. When a blessing is given, it's not a tangible object that you can see or touch, but an invisible shield that you must maintain to protect your relationships. When we truly honor these blessings, then they can negate our fears.

The sanctity of marriage is to love and honor one another. To love means to have "an intense feeling of deep affection" and to honor means to "regard with great respect" or "fulfill and keep (an agreement)." However, you don't need a marriage certificate or ceremony to uphold these blessings. It is an agreement that you choose to respect in your committed relationship.

On top of love and honor, there are seven blessings that are essential to practice in your relationship to make it a healthy and happy one.

**Commitment**: An unwavering choice you make to each other that requires dedication and discipline to have each other's best interests at heart.

**Encouragement**: Let uplifting words of kindness come out of your mouth to help build each other up.

**Faithfulness**: Always be firm in adhering to your promise of affection for one another so you may never need to stray.

**Forgiveness**: Forgive each other often and without apology before you go to bed at night.

**Peace**: Be calm in your disagreements and work together in harmony so each can be heard and understood.

**Understanding**: Be ready to listen so you can comprehend and gain understanding. Without it you won't be able to empathize and show compassion for one another.

**Wisdom**: Be wise in your discernment of what is true and good for you, your partner, and your relationship.

These blessings are tokens of knowledge that you can use to fight for the liveliness of your relationship. When you uphold these blessings in all your interactions with one another, you'll have a successful, loving relationship. You may want to make the vow of love but are not certain of how to navigate through the differences of personalities, or are too busy battling with the storms of life—now you know the little blessing reminders for everyday use.

Love is freely giving. You don't have to earn love and affection. You do not have to work *for* a relationship, though you do have to work hard *in* a relationship, especially when you need to grow together and walk towards a shared goal and vision for the betterment of it. One simple rule I have for couples in relationships is, if you don't grow together, you'll grow apart. If you don't walk together, you'll walk away from each other. The unconscious fear of rejection and abandonment are embedded in you and have wired your brain chemistry. You need to rewire it through your conscious choices and decisions. That's how you change yourself and gain the love of your life.

# 6

# Finding "Mr. Right" After Heartache

To love at all is to be vulnerable. Love anything and your heart will be wrung and possibly broken. If you want to make sure of keeping it intact you must give it to no one, not even an animal. Wrap it carefully round with hobbies and little luxuries; avoid all entanglements. Lock it up safe in the casket or coffin of your selfishness. But in that casket, safe, dark, motionless, airless, it will change. It will not be broken; it will become unbreakable, impenetrable, irredeemable.

—C.S. Lewis

WE LIVE IN a broken world. It's inevitable that we will get our hearts broken at one point or another. Nothing lasts forever here on earth. So it makes sense that to love is to be vulnerable.

Most people want to believe that love is easy—and it is (or at least, it should be). It is easy to love and give love. Love is freely given, or at least it needs to be. The problem is that people often mistake the meaning of love with having a successful relationship. To have a successful relationship, you'll need more than love. Love is essential but insufficient. A happy relationship requires the consistent investment of time, energy, effort, forgiveness, vulnerability, understanding, affection, and commitment. You shouldn't have to earn love, because when you do, it's no longer unconditional; but you do have work at your relationship.

I understand that most of us feel that we deserve to have a wonderful relationship with the love of our life, but it doesn't come on its own without our conscious choices. It requires active decision-making and participation, because there will be tough times. When you bring two individuals with similarities and differences together to work and function as a unit, friction occurs. We all hope to have the relationship run as smoothly and as happily as possible. That is where the challenges come into play, which require our dedication, devotion, and patience to overcome.

By the time we reach adulthood, most of us have had our hearts broken once or twice. Despite the reasons, we're left to pick up the pieces and mend them. It would be nice if we could be given a prognosis on how long it takes for the heart to heal. Unfortunately, there's no set time; like any wound, the bigger the injury, the longer it takes, and the bigger the scar will be.

You put a broken bone in a cast to help it heal; in a similar way, you also have to acknowledge that a broken heart is injured and needs tending to. You need to allow yourself to go through the pain and feel a gamut of emotions without lying to yourself.

Don't try to push these feelings down; they will only find ways to surface when you least want them to. You need to realize that all losses are painful. And you need to go through this grieving process for your loss. You wouldn't put a time limit on the grieving process for someone whose loved one just died, so don't beat yourself up for mourning the loss of a person you once loved. It would be easier to let go if the person has done you wrong or if the person is all bad, but that is rarely the case. This is someone you once cared deeply about with redeeming qualities. Therefore, it can be difficult to reconcile the conflicting emotions you have for the person after the breakup.

## THE FIVE STAGES OF GRIEVING

Grieving starts with denial, followed by anger, bargaining, depression, and finally acceptance. Don't expect yourself to go through this process in a linear fashion. You may find yourself jumping around those stages, and may even repeat some of them. It is perfectly fine when that happens; just allow yourself to go through the process as your heart needs to heal itself. I know it can be difficult to consciously allow yourself the time it takes to heal a broken heart. Most of us don't want to feel the pain of reliving the heartbreak or feel the pain of rejection over and over again. We end up occupying our time with temporary distractions and quick fixes, particularly if they can help us feel wanted again. This is easy when we have instant access to hundreds of people who are readily available and willing to get together for casual hookups.

### Jamie

Jamie, a client of mine, is a premed student in his third year at USC. When we talked about his love life, he pretty much said,

"I don't have time for love. It takes up too much time, especially when you start to get serious with a girl. You have to make time for her; otherwise she will get upset. You don't have to do that when you're just 'hanging out.' It's fun. You just hook up when you both have time, and then you go your separate ways. There's no expectations, no disappointment. No need for labels. That makes it less complicated." The mantra is fun, easy, and simple.

"Are the girls okay with this?" I asked.

"Yes, they're the same way. One of the girls I'm seeing is also premed and really busy, too. She calls me up at night sometimes. I don't mind being used." He chuckled, then continued, "I'm upfront with everyone at the beginning. We have this agreement. And if we really like each other, then we keep each other as the number one go-to person."

"Like friends with benefits?"

"Yes."

"What happens when one of you develops feelings for the other?"

"Then we can give it a try, but most of the time, we stop seeing each other. Because it doesn't work. That's why we have the contract in the first place."

Jamie truly believes he's taking this approach to relationships due to lack of time. He doesn't know what the future holds or where he's going for medical school, so logically, it seems to make sense. Whether Jamie is emotionally unavailable or has a fear of intimacy is a story that we'll have to get into later on, when he's ready to look at it. For now, he is consciously going into dating with his foot on the brake, trying to avoid the pain of possibly having to deal with a breakup. Most of us do this, not just young college students. The inevitability is that Jamie still experiences the pain nevertheless when he develops feelings for a girl and they have to stop seeing each other, but he's okay with it because the predictability of their contracted agreement is always in the forefront of his mind. He may experience the pain of loneliness because he doesn't allow himself to open up for love.

*Janet*

Janet is a divorced woman in her mid-30s. She wants to find a good man and have a partner for life, but she keeps getting hot and heavy with men who are not emotionally available. She blames it on the current culture of hookups. She likes the intensity of the relationships she has with these men; she finds them exciting. She recently met and dated a man on-and-off for about six months. During those six months, they broke up and got back together about four times. She is still holding onto him and believes that she can really make it work. She tells me that she is still in love with him and doesn't know why it's harder for her to let go of him than it was for her to let go of her ex-husband of ten years.

We dissected her life and relationships. She behaves the way she does with men in relationships because she is a Chaser with an anxious attachment style. So naturally, she craves the intimacy of a relationship, but feels that she has to earn it. She finds these relationships exciting and intense because she works hard to get the attention and affection of these men. It is exhilarating when she successfully gets the men who initially pushed her away. She's finally being desired and wanted. This accomplishment makes her feel important and worthwhile as a person, not to mention it is a challenge with the ultimate reward of acceptance and love once again.

As for the man she dated on and off for six months, he appears to be a Disrupter whose attachment style is disorganized. According to Janet, "When it is good, it is *really* good." What she forgets is the little black book full of women he cycles through when they're on breaks, the verbal venom they both spew at each other from time to time, and the physical altercations they have gotten into. The inconsistency of their relationship makes the future unpredictable. But its unpredictability creates anticipation, which can create excitement—particularly in Janet's case, who is yearning for the jackpot of "when it gets good" again. The reinforcement of positive intimacy she receives can be addicting, similar to someone who plays a slot machine or a drug addict chasing a high. Because people who play slot machines are *intermittently* rewarded, they don't know exactly when their reward is coming. They want to continuously invest their time (not to mention their money), thinking they will hit the jackpot at some point if they just play long enough. Also, it's harder for her to let him go than her husband because it hasn't fully run its course. Their relationship is constantly disrupted, and when something is incomplete, we have the need to follow through to see how it ends.

## THE FALLACY OF THINKING YOU WILL GET WHAT YOU DESERVE

Janet and Christy both want to be loved, but they have different comfort zones.

Christy has no tolerance for the anxiety she feels at the thought of having her flaws exposed and the possibility that she may be rejected. She packs up her bags and leaves before that can even happen, or else she sabotages herself by intentionally—or unintentionally, at times—pushing people away. Her motivation is to prevent others from seeing past her outward façade. Janet, on the other hand, has an incredibly high tolerance for anxiety, which in turn keeps her willing to fight for her relationships—even when they turn abusive.

Despite their differences, Janet and Christy share one common thread. Like many other individuals that I have come across, both inside and outside of my practice, they believe that they will simply "get" the partner they think they deserve. They think it will just magically "happen," without any work from them. Rather than working to improve themselves or address their issues, they spend their energy creating checklists of what they want and feel they deserve from a partner, hoping they will somehow attract that person to come into their life.

I hate to be the bearer of bad news, but this simply is not true. You don't just get the partner you think you deserve. We don't get what we want simply because we *think* we "deserve it." The truth of the matter is that we all deserve a wonderful partner, but the partner you unconsciously attract is one who complements your needs—both healthy and unhealthy. This person will be someone who shares a similar level of emotional development and differentiation, a person who may seem to be the missing piece to the jigsaw puzzle that is your life. But when you, yourself, are fundamentally broken, then that missing piece will only perfectly fit into the broken part of you. We all want a partner who is right *forever*, not just "right for now."

The question is, where are *you* currently at, emotionally?

## UNCONSCIOUS ATTRACTION

Are you happy and content with who you are as a person? Are you being kind and treating yourself the way you'd like others to treat you? Your unconscious attraction depends on this; the partner you attract is the one who will treat you the way you treat yourself. They will not treat you how you *want* to be treated or *think* you should be treated, so if you're not treating yourself like you're the queen of your universe, then don't expect to meet a guy who will treat you like a queen in his world.

Remember: if you possess a valuable item, you take good care of it. That way, when people see the level of attention and care you afford your valuable item, they're more likely to do the same if you ever let them borrow it.

## How Does Christy Believe She Should Be Treated?

Christy believes that she should be treated like a queen. At even the slightest hint of disappointment, she kicks the man out the door. In theory, this sounds fantastic; to a casual observer, it appears as though Christy is a really confident woman. But in reality, Christy's insecurities, though deeply buried, are readily apparent in her actions. She sees herself as someone who is not good enough, someone who is undesirable and unlovable to anyone who knows the truth about her. That's why she doesn't stay in a relationship for too long: if she stays, the other person will eventually see her for who she is, that part of her that she hides from everyone because she despises it herself. She also has an unconscious fear that her needs will not be fulfilled, and reasons that it's better to do the rejecting than being rejected; it's a bit less painful that way.

When Christy was finally able to see how she was operating based on her attachment style, she knew she needed to test out our theory and confront her fears. She needed to build up tolerance for discomfort, and so she delayed her impulse to leave the man she was dating and stayed in the relationship. Now, Christy doesn't run into relationships or trip over herself with infatuation. She has come to realize that love is more than seeing the attractiveness in another person; it's also accepting the blemishes. It may take time to build a strong, stable foundation, but Christy has chosen to walk and grow in love. She is learning to deal with disappointments and imperfections—both hers and as her partner's. More importantly, she allows her partner to see her flaws. That way, when he chooses to stay with her, she knows that he has accepted her, flaws and all.

## AND HOW ABOUT JANET?

As for Janet, it's not really possible to undo or reduce her tolerance for anxiety-producing relationships. This is a fortitude that has been built up over the years, but luckily, there's no real need to tear down those walls, provided Janet understands that she tends to attract men who are Runners. So long as she bears this in mind, they can do the approach-avoidance dance, she can pursue him for his love and affection, or she can learn to let go of a guy for his disorganized attachment style.

The real problem is that these types of attachment styles feed into Janet's unhealthy needs. She feels the need to chase and pursue potential partners; to her mind, it makes the relationship more worthwhile and exciting when she finally achieves it. But when she meets a Keeper, someone who is good for her *and* accepting of her, she sees that person as not good enough and flawed. When she gives a Keeper a chance, she finds that person less exciting over time, because she gets used to the "normalcy" of a safe, secure, and loving partner. And so she leaves the man and the relationship.

Why is this? To understand this, we must understand how Janet's self-image affects her perception of others. Because Janet sees herself as not being good enough, it follows that only flawed people or people who are also not good enough would be able to accept her for who she is. By contrast, people who *are* good enough or more than good enough would naturally make her work for it.

As human beings, we instinctively want to make progress and move forward. We want the best things in life and we believe we deserve them. We are superego-driven; when someone is better than us, then we believe that person is good for us because we deserve the best. When someone is accepting of us, it can only mean that they're inferior to us and should be rejected.

These toxic relationship patterns can be very addicting. It's like a roller coaster ride, full of twists and turns. What keeps you engaged in this cycle of toxicity is the dopamine that is released when you feel you're being rewarded. When you work really hard at something and you get rewarded for it, you are ecstatic. You value the reward more highly for the hard work it represents. You feel recognized and validated for the hard work you put in.

But if you keep getting rewarded every day for your effort, your appreciation for your reward will lessen daily. Eventually, your reward will stop affecting you and lose its meaning. Your prize is no longer rewarding because what was once special has now become normal. Because of this, your brain stops releasing dopamine. The ups and downs that had once added "color" to the relationship are gone.

What Janet needs to learn is that you don't need *negativity* to make a relationship dynamic. You can create your own excitement with *positivity*. That's why it's important to learn to recognize some of the signs of healthy and unhealthy relationships so you'll be able to see the red flags or better evaluate your relationship dynamics.

| HEALTHY LOVE | UNHEALTHY LOVE |
|---|---|
| You allow each other room for each other's individuality and identity so you can each be "yourself" | You feel pressure to change to meet partner's standard or live up to partner's expectation |
| You bring out each other's best qualities | You are fearful of being judged or being critical of partner |
| You allow for changes in the relationship and encourage each other for positive growth | You are fearful of changes and have the needs to remain the same but feel stuck and stagnant |
| You feel good about yourself | You look towards your partner for validation or reassurance and rely on partner's approval for self-worth |
| You openly listen to partner's thoughts, feelings, desires and needs | You feel defensive and feel the need to shut down and shut partner out |
| You do not try to change or control your partner | You focus on partner's shortcoming and feel the need to change them |
| You allow time for the relationship to slowly develop | You manipulate or force intimacy to take place |
| You do not withhold love and affection during conflict | You are emotionally unavailable and punitive |
| You are open to receiving and giving without expectation | You are fearful of losing yourself in a relationship or getting too close |
| You take care of yourself and are responsible for your own happiness in a relationship | You need your partner to feel whole and rely on partner to make you happy |

| You are willing and happy to commit to each other | You remain distant and refuse to commit or feel suffocated/consumed by partner |
| You are willing to forgive each other | You hold grudges and try to "guilt-trip" partner |
| You are able to confront and communicate problems with each other and work together towards solution | You avoid conflicts or violently fight with each other |
| You are open to feedback without being defensive or argumentative | You are dismissive of partner or put your partner down |
| You have mutual respect of each other's thoughts feelings and boundaries | You unilaterally make decisions and control everything without discussing with partner |
| You allow and respect each other's space and privacy | You don't have personal space or have to share everything with partner |
| You feel safe and secure enough to be vulnerable | You find your partner and the relationship unpredictable and unstable |
| You trust each other as well as yourself | You lie to each other and yourself or find yourself making excuses |
| You are supportive of each other when face with problems | You blame your partner when things go wrong |
| You respect each other's personal interests, hobbies and activities | You are easily jealous and hurt, in need of constant attention with little time apart from each other |

| You feel closer to each other as your relationship has gotten stronger over time | You feel that your relationship is getting weaker and you're more distant from each other |
| --- | --- |

## How to Curb Negative Behavior and Find Your Knight in Shining Armor

If we want to find the Mr. Right who's right forever, and not just right now, then there are a number of changes we have to make. We must stop spending so much time distracting ourselves with seasonal flings. We need to allow ourselves time to heal when we're hurt, especially after a breakup, so that we don't carry our baggage from one relationship to another. Engaging in a relationship with someone who intermittently gives us love and affection is giving into our unhealthy desires, which does more harm than good. We need to let go of our façade and be true to ourselves. We need to learn to fall in love with ourselves so that we can allow others to fall in love with us. We need to truly believe our true self is good enough to be accepted and appreciated.

Many of us want to believe that dating is a game, a question of making the right moves when you meet someone you really like. But love is not a game. Remember, all games must eventually come to an end, but you want to make your true love last a lifetime. With that goal in mind, you need to build a solid foundation from the get-go. And like anything built to stand the test of time, it first needs time to cultivate. So don't be too quick with your dismissal at your prospect's minor flaws. No one is perfect, yourself included. But we can *create* our perfect relationship; by knowing that you're worthy of love, you allow another person to accept the best version of yourself that you are and will ever become.

# 7

# *The Love You Show*

Love never dies a natural death. It dies because
we don't know how to replenish its sources. It
dies of blindness and errors and betrayals. It
dies of illness and wounds; it dies of weariness,
of withering, of tarnishing.

—ANAIS NIN

### LOVE IS NOT A CHANCE—LOVE IS A *CHOICE*

"I DIDN'T THINK I was ready for marriage, but it was time for
me to get out of my parents' house. I was so young; I was only
eighteen. I hardly knew anything about life or love," says Angie.

Angie is a seventy-three-year-old widow. Most young adults
today would consider hers the "old generation," from a time
when life was much different compared to today. Angie came

We expect them to live up to our expectations. But with every expectation, there's a great chance for disappointment.

Angie came to realize that disappointment in her relationship. The major decision, to get married, was fine; as she said, they were aligned in the important things. It was in the tiny, daily tasks that problems began to emerge. She didn't fold his laundry the way he wanted. He wasn't the handyman she had expected him to be. More and more disappointments and frustrations began to set in as each person failed to live up to the other's expectations.

Angie still recalls the first major fight they had as a newlywed couple. She can remember vividly how their relationship wasn't the same as it used to be. He wasn't patiently consoling her; he didn't gently wipe away the tears on her face when she was sad, like he did during their courtship. Instead, he yelled back and eventually left her alone in the house. She felt distraught and defeated, thinking that Jimmy was not the man she thought he was—that he was not the man she married. He didn't care about her; how could he leave her in tears if he did? Worse, she questioned the life expectancy of their marriage. Was it going to last? Did she marry the wrong man?

"He was gone for a really long time," Angie recalled. "I'm not sure how long, but it was long enough for me to scrub every corner and crevice in the kitchen and bathroom. The toilets sparkled by the time I was done." She chuckled before continuing, "Then he came home with a small bouquet of flowers. While I was cleaning, I'd conjured up so many scenarios of how it was going to play out, but that wasn't one of them. He didn't say much. He didn't even say, 'Sorry.' All he said was, 'I bought you these,' and handed them to me.

"I was still hurt and angry. A part of me wanted to throw the flowers at him or dump them in the trash. I knew that would make it worse, but I wasn't ready to give him the satisfaction of thinking that everything would be okay by accepting the flowers and thanking him for them. I told him to put them on the table. I didn't run to get the vase and put them in water as I would normally do. I took my time putting away my cleaning supplies and did everything else I could think of before I put them in water."

"What happened afterward?" I asked.

"We eventually talked. One rule that we applied then and until the very end was from that one Bible verse: 'Do not let the sun set upon your anger.' We made sure from that day on that every argument was resolved before we went to bed. If not, we agreed to revisit the next day to have it resolved. And we tried not to withhold affection from each other in the meantime."

Angie didn't have the psychological knowledge or background to explain everything that happened in her story. But she beautifully displayed how love operates in a long-lasting relationship and the emotional intricacies that are involved.

A loving relationship is not free of differences. Where there are differences, there will be disagreements. How you decide to deal with these disagreements can either be constructive, which brings you closer to your love, or destructive, which will pull you further away from one another.

## WHAT BROUGHT ANGIE AND JIMMY CLOSER TOGETHER?

Angie and Jimmy had different ideas of their roles as husband and wife, and they also had different expectations of how each should be treated. They soon learned to manage their expectations of each other, to be more appreciative rather than expectant. Whether by choice or chance (perhaps a little of both), they stumbled onto each other's "love language," though they didn't put a name to it.

According to Gary Chapman, there are five love languages. Knowing your love language can help you communicate to your partner exactly how you'd like to be loved. This is crucial in keeping your relationship alive. Our hope is to have a soulmate who understands, supports, and loves us unconditionally, someone who knows us in a way that no one else does. Our soulmate knows the right thing to say and do to make us feel special, as if he or she could read our mind. All of this is possible if you know the *secret*.

## THE SECRET

The *secret* of getting exactly what you want ... *is asking for it*. Even though our partners are our soulmates, they still don't possess the ability to read our minds. Unless we tell them, they'll never know what we desire. We can choose to squirrel away our desires and hope that our partner will stumble onto it, like Angie and Jimmy did. But you may not be lucky enough to find it early in a relationship. You may end up going a lifetime without getting the love you wanted. Knowing your love language and letting your partner know what it is takes the guesswork out of the equation. When you inform each other how you would like to be loved, it leaves no room for assumptions and disappointments. Oftentimes, we're inclined to give love the only way we know how, or the way we want to be loved. We use the golden rule as a model: "Do unto others as you would have them do unto you." It feels good when we give.

Unfortunately, when we give we make it about us instead of the receiver. We give what we want to give, not what the receiver wants. We also give what we want to receive. We don't necessarily give love the way our partner needs it. When you think or say to your partner, "You should know how to love me," you're at risk of having your partner love you according to his or her own needs, not yours.

Let's take a look and find out which of the following love languages speaks to your heart.

## THE FIVE LOVE LANGUAGES

*Love Language #1: Words of Affirmation*
You may have heard the adage, "Actions speak louder than words," but this is not always the case. Language is one of the ways for us to express our thoughts, feelings, and affections for each other. We all know the warm feeling that comes from someone giving you a compliment, acknowledging your hard work, or saying, "I love you." These are all examples of "words of affirmation."

Words of affirmation are any verbal expression that communicates love, affection, appreciation, dedication, and assurance to your partner. For some people, words of affirmation don't do anything, as they're able to provide them for themselves. For others, receiving words of affirmation will send their spirits to the moon and make their hearts dance with joy. It particularly provides validation and assurance in situations where insecurities commonly arise. People who have words of affirmation as their love language tend to be sensitive to words. As verbal affection sends you to the moon, insults can shatter their heart to pieces.

*Love Language #2: Physical Touch*
When words of affirmation are your love language, you tend to be more careful with your words. If your partner's love language is *physical touch*, he might not be as selective with his words, and he may not give you much verbal affirmation. He will instead be "touchy" as his way of displaying affection.

As I mentioned earlier, we tend to give love the way we know how or the way we want to receive it. When someone's love language is physical touch, they may assume that it is also yours. When they display physical affection, they may think they are communicating love in lieu of words. He may think that he is saying it loud and clear with his actions; after all, if he didn't care and love you, then he wouldn't want to touch you.

From this example, you can see how not knowing your partner's love language can lead to a huge problem in a relationship. I can't think of a bigger issue than thinking that your partner doesn't love you, and if you don't interpret his casual contact as an expression of love, you may feel as though he cares nothing for you. You won't feel fulfilled, and vice versa. By knowing each other's love language, you can let your partner know so he can make more of a conscious effort to communicate with you in that way.

### Love Language #3: Quality Time

If you think about it, time is probably one of the most valuable commodities that we have. When you give your time to someone, you're giving a part of your life away that you can never have back. But it's not just the time—it's the *quality of the time.*

Quality time is not merely being in the same room together. What I hear from some couples is, "We spend so much time together. We live together; we see each other every day. I come straight home from work, so I don't understand why she says we don't spend enough time together."

Quality time is determined by your intention and purpose—the time you set aside to spend with each other, as well as the undivided attention you give one another. Quality time is about having a schedule full of activities and responsibilities but still making time for your loved one. It doesn't need to be an elaborate date or a fancy sit-down with a seven-course dinner where you have a heart-to-heart conversation. It can simply be fifteen minutes to check in with your partner to see how they're doing, a few hours to see a movie together, or taking the time out of your busy day to sit together with a cup of tea or coffee, watching the world go by in silence. Again, the activity varies, but what remains constant is the intention of connecting and giving your partner your undivided attention.

I know most of us feel that we live in a fast-paced environment that demands the efficient use of our time. We need to multitask to get as much done as possible. Perhaps that's precisely the reason why spending quality time together can help someone feel very loved. You're not trying to kill two birds with one stone. The person is not only your *top* priority; in that given time, your partner is your *only* priority. When you give your partner time and attention, what you're saying is, "You matter." What could be a better way to say "I love you" than by making them feel that they're the only thing that matters in the world, at least for that moment in time?

### Love Language #4: Acts of Service

For some people, love speaks to them in a more practical sense. These people don't need quality time or verbal reassurances; what brings music to their ears is hearing you say, "Let me do that for you," and following through on it. This love language is called *acts of service*.

Angie never had to pump gas again after her huge fight with Jimmy. You may have thought that perhaps their love language was words of affirmation, because they both wanted to talk after they fought. In fact, when they finally talked that day after their fight, Angie told Jimmy that she appreciated the flowers, but that it didn't do anything for her. The flowers were going to die in a few days, and then she would just have to clean up the mess.

She wanted Jimmy to help her out more around the house. Why do you think she went and gave the house a good scrub down? It was certainly a productive way to channel her anger, but it wasn't because she enjoyed it; it needed to be done.

Angie's love language was acts of service. Once she told Jimmy that and what it meant to her, he discovered more ways to express his love for her over their lifetime together. He would do the vacuuming without being asked, take out the garbage when he saw it was full, and the gas tank was never empty when she got in the car.

The problem most couples face is that they feel like their partner is not doing enough. Oftentimes, this isn't strictly true—they do more than enough—it's just not what you wanted. A little effort will go a long way *if* you know what you are doing. When you speak your partner's language, they'll start noticing more of the "right" things you do instead of focusing on the "wrongs."

### *Love Language #5: Receiving Gifts*

Perhaps you can guess what Jimmy's love language was? Remember, we tend to give love the way we want to receive it, instead of how our partner wants it.

With that in mind, it makes perfect sense that Jimmy's love language was *receiving gifts*. That's why Jimmy went out and got her flowers; it was his way of telling her that he cares. He assumed that she would love receiving little gifts like flowers because that's how *he* wants to be loved.

Receiving gifts is not about the materialistic aspect of the gift or its monetary value, but more so the idea behind the gifts. It's the thoughtfulness and effort that goes into getting what your partner likes. For Jimmy, he found it endearing when Angie thought of him when she was at the grocery store and picked up his favorite treats. It's the notion that he was known and cared for by his partner and that she thinks of him in his absence. She buys little gifts to remind him that she loves him and thinks of him when he's not around. The gift-giving love language is bringing you happiness in a little box.

Soulmates don't necessarily know everything about each other when they choose each other. They may never know everything about one another; people are continuously growing and changing, and what was known yesterday may be different today. The difference is, soulmates keep each other informed of these fresh developments. They do not expect their partners to have mind-reading abilities, and they do not expect their partners to fulfill all of their wants and needs. They make note of their partner's love language, and speak to them in words (or gifts or actions) that they understand and appreciate. The key to building a happy relationship is recognizing your partner's effort and showing gratitude and appreciation, not expectation.

That said, it is important to keep in mind that you must also know your *own* love language. Like any other essential need in your life, you must learn to give yourself the love you want. Even though you and your partner may know each other's love languages, it's doesn't guarantee that you'll be one hundred percent fulfilled by your partner. What you need to do is fulfill at least eighty percent of your wants and needs yourself, and leave it to your partner to top you off.

Your soulmate is your best friend, your confidant, and your lover—essentially your other half, who seeks to understand, support, and nurture the growth of their relationship with you. When you're able to fulfill your own desires and have a partner who is also attentive to your needs, you'll feel invigorated, rejuvenated, and on top of the world. After all, you give your best when you're at your best. When you feel loved and nurtured in your relationship, you want to give the same in return; when you love someone, you want to speak their love language. I'd imagine your partner will appreciate how romantic you are by trying to keep the relationship alive, especially when you choose to show them each and every day that they are loved, wanted, thought of, and important to you. Let your partner know how important your relationship is to you. That's ultimately what we all want in life—to know that we're loved and we're significant to someone else.

*Exercise: Honey Jar*

A simple exercise that I have couples do is to implement a concept called "Honey Jar." On small pieces of paper, write down different things that you and your partner want. Then, both you and your partner need to fill up two separate jars with the small pieces of paper you wrote on. Each week, you and your partner should pick one piece out of the other's jar and fulfill what is being said.

This exercise helps partners to meet each other's needs while gaining an opportunity to show your love for one another.

# 8

# We Fight to Communicate

He is not perfect. You aren't either, and the two of you will never be perfect. But if he can make you laugh at least once, causes you to think twice, and if he admits to being human and making mistakes, hold onto him and give him the most you can. He isn't going to quote poetry, he's not thinking about you every moment, but he will give you a part of him that he knows you could break. Don't hurt him, don't change him, and don't expect for more than he can give. Don't analyze. Smile when he makes you happy, yell when he makes you mad, and miss him when he's not there. Love hard when there is love to be had. Because perfect guys don't exist, but there's always one guy that is perfect for you.

— BOB MARLEY

## ARE YOU WILLING TO FIGHT
## FOR YOUR RELATIONSHIP?

It may sound hard to believe, but it's true—successful relationships involve a lot of fighting!

Happy couples fight for their relationships, certainly, but they also fight *in* their relationships. Thankfully, when you're willing to fight for your relationship, then you're able to survive the fights you'll have in your relationship. The question is, are you willing to fight for your relationship? If so, at what cost? How far are you willing to go?

Let me make one thing perfectly clear: I am *not* telling you to stay in an abusive relationship because you believe you have to fight for it. True love nurtures and promotes the well-being of both partners and the relationship itself. Abuse is the opposite of caring and nurturing—it doesn't matter what the person says. We all get angry and may say hurtful words at times, but you can learn to handle your emotions more effectively. The question we're asking (and answering) here is, "Are you willing to stand up and fight for your love and your relationship?"

*Lily and Joe*

It may be a cliché, but the jokes about one's in-laws are probably as old as human civilization.

Lily and Joe are one of my favorite interracial couples. Joe's mom is not very fond of Lily because she's not Italian and could never cook Joe's favorite dish (ossobuco). Joe doesn't mind that Lily doesn't make ossobuco like his mother; as a matter of fact, he loves showing off his talents in the kitchen in front of his wife. It's one of their quality times together. They don't just cook together; they make an event out of it. She puts on the music, he opens a bottle of wine, she helps him with preparation, he shows her how to slice and dice properly, he sings, and she laughs. They have a great time in the kitchen.

Except when Joe's mother comes to town.

"Did you know that I'm banned from my kitchen when she's in town?" Lily asked me. "She has a way of making me feel really insecure in my own house," she added, frowning.

Joe turned to Lily, saying, "You know, she does the same to me, too."

"So, neither of you are allowed in the kitchen when she's there?" I asked.

"Yes. That's my mom's way of telling us that she cares. She makes my favorite dishes and does all of the cooking and cleaning. She is just trying to make our lives easier," Joe responded.

"You always try to defend her. When do you ever stand up for me?" Lily asked, interrupting.

"How often does she come, and how long does she stay?" I asked.

"She stays for about a week, and she comes twice a year," Lily answered.

"Does she know she makes you feel insecure?" I inquired.

"No!" Lily snapped back.

I turned to Joe and asked, "Do you know how Lily feels when your mother is there?"

"I didn't know about her insecurity. I knew she was not too happy, since it is a bit cramped for all of us to be in our small apartment, but I didn't think she would be this upset," Joe said.

## PERSPECTIVE AND PERCEPTION

As humans, we have a natural tendency to make assumptions to complete a picture. We have difficulty dealing with what is not resolved or incomplete; we feel the need to fill in the gaps in order to process and understand the situation.

Our assumptions are typically based on our perception. Unfortunately, our perception is not always accurate; oftentimes, it's distorted based on the color of the lens we're looking through, both literally and figuratively. Just like a coin, there are two sides to every story. The problem is that when we assume, we believe the other side of the coin is the same as the side we see.

Everyone has perception, but not everyone has perspective. When you see something from your point of view, that is your *perception*. Having *perspective* is when you're able to see the other side of the coin. You're able to stand where the other person stands and see what the other person is seeing. This enables you to understand the other person's side of the story as well as yours, providing for a complete picture.

In our earlier example, Lily assumed that Joe would know how she felt when Joe's mother came to town. Joe, on the other hand, assumed that he already knew how she felt. To address this issue, we worked to eliminate assumptions as much as possible, leaving very little room for guessing in their communication when it came to what they wanted and how they could build a successful, happy relationship.

The next time Joe's mother came to stay, they were more prepared than ever. They had the basic tools to work together, were set to be more communicative with each other, and learn to set boundaries with the in-laws. They agreed that it would be nice to get out of the house and not just have Joe's mother cooking the whole time she was there. That would also allow Lily to get back into the kitchen, rather than being banned from it during the visit. Lily planned a nice evening where they would all go out for dinner. Joe told his mother of Lily's plan, and reservations were made at the best Italian restaurant in town.

The night of their outing, Joe and Lily came home from work to find Joe's mother in the kitchen, making her famous ossobucco. Lily pulled her husband into their bedroom to communicate her frustration.

"I don't understand why she is cooking. We told her about the dinner reservation for tonight. What are we going to do?" Lilly posed the question.

Joe knew he had a crucial decision to make. If he told his mom to wait and have her cook the next day, she would be upset and disappointed. But if they stayed at home, his wife would not be happy. Deep down, he knew what he needed to do to protect his marriage. And while some tears were shed that night, Joe figured that it was his father's responsibility to wipe away his mother's tears.

They managed to clean everything up and get to their dinner on time. Surprisingly, everyone warmed up and had a great time toward the end of the evening.

Joe joked in their follow-up session, "We're Italian; there's nothing can't be solved after a couple of bottles of wine." But in reality, this was no easy task for Joe; especially in an Italian family, you don't disappoint mom!

## How Often Do You Fight in Your Relationship?

How often do you fight in your relationship? And do you want to have those fights?

I'd imagine that, like most couples, you probably answered no to that last question. None of us want to have quarrels and quandaries in our relationships. Many of us shy away from the idea of having arguments, fights, confrontations, or whatever word you use in dealing with conflicts. They are deemed as bad or negative; they mean "your relationship is on the rocks."

But what if I were to tell you that having conflicts in your relationship is not necessarily bad? In fact, conflicts and confrontations can bring greater understanding. We all want peace, not pain, but rainbows only come after the rain.

So long as you still have the will to fight, it means you still have passion for your relationship. It means you still care. If you were resigned to your situation, you wouldn't waste your energy fighting with each other. How we channel this passion productively is the real question worth exploring. But before we get into that, let's figure out what causes the fights in your relationship. It's almost impossible to have two persons living in the same household without there being some conflicts. And if you don't think you have any conflicts, it could be you're not looking hard enough at your relationship, or you're just avoiding them.

## What Are Your Triggers?

Do you know what gets you riled up?

A good starting point to determine which buttons you don't want pushed is by examining your family of origin. When fighting with other family members, what is the fight usually about? What bothers you about other people in your interpersonal relationships? Carl Jung once said, "Everything that irritates us about others can lead us to an understanding of ourselves." Unfortunately, for most people, what irritates them leads to destruction instead of understanding because of their emotional reaction. Learning to identify our hot buttons and taking ownership of them can help minimize our reactions. When you take ownership of your own shortcomings, you can improve them. You're also less likely to project them onto others; *projection* is when we magnify in others what we consciously (or unconsciously) do not like about ourselves.

Let's take Lily and Joe as an example. Remember the two statements from Lily: "You always try to defend her. When do you ever stand up for me?" I didn't focus on those sentences when she first verbalized them, as it would have been a distraction from our initial conversation, but the sentiment itself was so profound that I later invited them to revisit it.

In the final review, the statements weren't entirely accurate. Joe doesn't "always" defend his mother. Her second point, "When do you ever stand up for me?" was almost certainly a rhetorical question, because any answers Joe provided would not suffice. This is because the issue was one of projection; what Lily didn't like about Joe already exists in her. She's mad that Joe doesn't defend her because she is not able to stand up for herself or Joe against her own father. She's upset with her own cowardice, but is not able to recognize that, and therefore takes it out on Joe.

Lily's father thinks that Joe's profession (a chef) means he is not good enough for her. Her father has said, "If he wants to be in the restaurant industry, he should at least be an owner." He thought she should have married someone with more prestige, like a doctor, a lawyer, or a businessman like himself. Every time her father brings it up, Lily just keeps quiet, all the while hating herself for doing so. When Joe doesn't stand up to his mother, she in turn thinks that he is weak, which is the one trait she loathes about herself.

When we're able to recognize the projections in our relationships, we learn to have more understanding of ourselves and our partner's role as a catalyst. Salt doesn't sting unless there's an open wound. We need to acknowledge and accept our own flaws so we can facilitate meaningful conversation and connection. I know—it is easier said than done. It can take a lifetime of introspection and reflection to know everything we need to know about ourselves, from a conscious to an unconscious level. But even a journey of a thousand miles starts with a single step. While you're working on knowing your own projections, there are a few things you can practice to ensure the fights in your relationship become more constructive.

## The Art of Communication

How is the communication in your relationship? Are you communicating in a way that your partner responds to?

Again, let's use Lily's statements as an example: "You always try to defend her. When do you ever stand up for me?" Can you spot what can be improved in these statements?

First, she starts off with a "you," which can prompt the listener to raise his guard and become more defensive, and therefore be less inclined to take in what the other person has to say. When you start with a "you," it insinuates that you're blaming the other person by pointing the proverbial finger at them. When we feel blamed or attacked, we have a tendency to defend ourselves, which shifts the focus to clearing our names rather than hearing what the other person has to say. This in turn creates frustration in the person doing the talking, because they feel they are not being heard.

Second, Lily said, "You always..." Have you ever paid attention to the language that you use on a daily basis? If you haven't, I want you to start being mindful of the language you use to see how often you use these types of absolute terms, such as "all," "always," "every," "never," "none," and so on. The truth of the matter is, we don't live in a black-and-white world. There are many more colors in our thinking than an all-or-nothing mentality can encompass. The next time you're thinking in absolute terms, consider replacing those words with terms like: *many, most, some, often, frequently, usually, generally, sometimes, few, rarely, sporadically,* or *seldom.* These words tend to be a bit more accurate and objective, and hopefully easier on the ears of listeners, as well.

Third, she asked a question without any intention of hearing an answer. Half of good communication is listening skills. Most of the time, we tend to listen for the purposes of reacting, rather than understanding.

I want you to imagine that communication is a game. There's an exercise I often have my audience do as an icebreaker when I give talks or workshops called Two Truths and a Lie. The idea of the game is to come up with two truths and a lie about yourself, with the hope of making your lie as convincing as your truths. As a listener, you have to differentiate the truths from the lie by asking questions. I want you to imagine having a conversation with your partner with this concept in mind. As a listener, you won't jump at every opportunity to interrupt your partner and cut off the conversation, because an investigator must ask questions and gather all information before coming to a conclusion.

The art of communication lies more in the listening part. In order to actively listen, you need to remain silent. Silence is a wonderful technique that not enough people make use of. I'm not talking about giving your partner the silent treatment (unless you need your space and time to collect your thoughts, process your feelings, and put them together more coherently for your partner). Silence within the context of a dialogue is needed for you to hear and think about what the person has said. The silence will also give the speaker an opportunity to reflect on what was said. A lot of times, the speaker is able to catch and correct him- or herself. It may be a cliché, but silence *is* golden. If the speaker fails to reflect on what was said, the silence can also help you, the listener, reflect and seek clarification.

*Reflection* and *clarification* also works both ways, as a speaker and as a listener. If you master the basic skills of using "I" statements, giving each other enough silence for reflecting, and seeking clarification in your daily conversation, you'll minimize the number of the fights in your relationship.

Let's put this into practice using Lily's statements from before: "You always try to defend her. When do you ever stand up for me?"

From a communicator point of view, Lily could have a softer start that won't lead into an argument by changing the statement into an "I" statement. For example: "I feel sad and disappointed when you defend your mom before hearing my side." This statement will more than likely prompt Joe to ask for Lily's side of the story.

However, let's say that Lily still begins her statements harshly. Joe could easily get defensive and point the finger at Lily for what she has done wrong in the past, which only adds fuel to the fire. The more baggage that gets dragged into the argument, the quicker we get off-track from the original point. What Joe could do is implement the *clarification technique*. Clarification techniques require two essential components to clear out the issues: *acknowledgement* and *validation*. People often mistake acknowledgement or validation for admitting fault. On the contrary, it simply means you're demonstrating that you understand what has been said and you've received it without defense or judgement. For example: "What I'm hearing is, you think I defend my mother too much and don't do it enough for you?"

This helps Lily feel heard and understood, and also diffuses the situation, which creates space for them to come up with a solution together. Most disagreements turn into fights because we act on our emotions instead of honestly communicating our feelings, and we don't know how to defuse the situation. Oftentimes, you're caught at a bad time and a bad place. When you need to have a serious conversation, it helps to schedule a time when you are both in a good head space to talk. Try to avoid having a serious conversation when you're hungry, tired, or late at night. You want to have enough time to get the issues resolved.

I recognize that old habits die hard. It takes time to practice and learn new techniques to improve your communication. Unfortunately, we tend to focus more on the negative than the positive. That's why I'm asking you to make a conscious effort to give each other a break. Be the cheerleader when you and your partner make an attempt. We learn better with positive reinforcement.

## How Do You Handle Conflict?

Until you've mastered the art of communication, chances are some of your discussions will still turn into fights.

The question is, when a fight breaks out, how do you typically handle it?

We all have our own ways of handling conflicts. These depend on our capacity to tolerate uncomfortable feelings and on our attachment styles. We have already discussed attachment in intimacy; our personality in intimacy correlates to how we handle the intense emotions of conflicts. It is important to identify what type of a person you are in a fight. It's equally important to recognize your partner's tendency. The problem isn't so much knowing which type of a person you are as it is failing to recognize the differences between you and your partner.

Generally speaking, there are four types of personalities operating in a fight. Which one of the following are you? Are you a charger, a runner, a soother, or a combination of all three?

## The "Chargers"

*Chargers* tend to be reactive. They are emotionally strong and get very invested in a fight. They want to confront the problem immediately, here and now. They want to get to the bottom of it at all cost. Their tempers may rise and their voices might go up an octave or two.

They're the people who act on anything, at anytime, anywhere, as long as they can get to the bottom of something. They have a sense of urgency to get conflict resolved quickly, and sometimes their timing can be awful. They may have a fear that if things don't get resolved there and then, they will never be resolved. After all, a fight without immediate resolution may mean the end of a relationship; the person will leave and never come back. At least, that's how the Charger sees things.

On the flip side, when you sense that it's not going your way or not having the immediate resolution you want, a Charger is the first to resign and call it quits. Remember: each time you verbalize "let's break up" in a disagreement, you weaken the strength of your relationship.

This type of fighting style is common among those with the trait of anxious attachment, due to their fear of abandonment. As a Pursuer in intimacy, you're a Charger in a disagreement. But this ends up being counterproductive. When you're emotionally charged, you're not rational or logical. You're not effective in communicating what you think and how you feel. You may not get your point across, and you might even become an attacker. You're not able to use "I" statements or reflect on your own thought processes. If you identify yourself as a Charger, it helps to create a space where you can calm down and collect your thoughts before addressing the issues. Otherwise, your partner may get scared and need to escape from you. When that happens, you may end up interpreting it as abandonment.

But not everyone can tolerate the tension Chargers create, and may feel the need to just get away. This brings us to the "Escapers."

## THE "ESCAPERS"

*Escapers* have a need to avoid and run away from conflicts. They'll either literally walk away from a fight or figuratively go into their own world for the time being. They have difficulty tolerating tension and the feelings that arise from conflict. They disengage by shutting down and shutting you out. They may not be able to hear what you have to say because they're too occupied with their own thoughts and feelings. Escapers hope and believe the problem will go away if they ignore it and believe that the problem will take care of itself with the passing of enough time, a classic example of the "sweep it under the rug" analogy. Escapers tend to give you the silent treatment until enough time has passed or the tension has subsided inside of them. Then they'll be back to normal, going about their day like nothing has happened. However, while they may have returned to a physiological state of equilibrium, the conflict remains, with its feelings unresolved. It is important for Escapers to delay their running and build up a tolerance for their discomfort of emotions. They need to commit themselves to return to dealing with the problems with a calm state of being.

Can you guess which type of attachment style they most likely have? If you guessed avoidant attachment, or a Runner, then you're correct. Runners and Escapers are essentially two sides of the same coin, with avoidance as their primary defense mechanism. They try to run and escape from intense feelings, whether positive or negative. This behavior keeps repeating until there are layers of unresolved emotions built up over years. This is problematic, particularly with unpleasant feelings, because as the pressure of hurt and anger accumulates, things will eventually erupt like a volcano.

## THE "SOOTHERS"

*Soothers* try to defuse the situation. They can talk things out calmly or take a quick break if that makes the conversation more constructive. They're flexible in their ways of dealing with conflicts. These individuals tend to be Keepers who are more securely attached, though anxious attachment individuals can sometimes adopt this strategy due to their anxiety, trying to appease and please their partner for fear they might leave. The difference is securely-attached Soothers can communicate their thoughts and feelings while being logical and rational. Their focus is on comforting their partners and trying to help their partners get their needs met as well as theirs because they know how it feels to have their own needs met.

It's wonderful to be in a relationship with a securely-attached Soother, especially when you can accept it. On the other hand, anxious Soothers are motivated out of fear. They feel that they need to appease the situation or their partner will abandon them. It is important for anxious Soothers to keep their emotions in check so they don't continually appease their partners while ignoring their own needs. Otherwise, they may end up feeling angry, resentful, and neglected because their emotions and needs aren't being taken care of.

## A COMBINATION OF THE THREE

If you're a Disrupter with disorganized attachment who doesn't have self-control, then you'll likely find yourself cycling through all of these without any clear or consistent strategy. In an abusive relationship, this is what's typically referred to as the honeymoon cycle. It has a build-up phase, followed by the beat-up, and finally the make-up phase. This is the most dangerous and unhealthy way of dealing with conflicts, one which requires serious professional help to successfully resolve.

## DEALING WITH THE MATCH-UPS

We all have different ways of handling conflict and varying capacities to tolerate tension. We also have different ways of processing information. Some of us need to communicate our thoughts and feelings right away; others need to collect their thoughts and calm themselves instead of spewing venom in anger. Whichever your usual approach is, at the end of the day, we need to effectively communicate to see eye-to-eye.

**Some of the practical questions that you can use to start creating a helpful dialogue are:**

1. What are you feeling?

    a. What I'm hearing is...

    b. What is it that I'm not getting?

2. What do you need?

    a. Do you need a hug?

    b. Do you need to have your space?

3. How can I help?

    a. What can I do for you right now to help you feel better?

We must learn to meet each other halfway. Trying to force your partner to meet you where you are to take care of your feelings is probably not going to work. These questions can help you understand where your partner is at emotionally, and their current needs. At the same time, it allows your partner to learn to communicate their needs. This doesn't leave you feeling helpless and leaves your partner feeling cared for. And remember, there are ways for any type to interact with any other type. A Charger may feel that having a Soother as a partner is a good idea, but in the heat of the moment, you two will have little ability to influence each other, as there is a great deal of emotional tension and very little positive sentiment (unless you allow for it). A Soother paired with a Runner with a tendency to avoid tension will create an overwhelming dynamic. A Runner with a Charger is probably the worst pairing, as it creates a cat-and-mouse game with a vicious cycle of a Runner/Pursuer dynamic. Knowing your personality traits can help you monitor your behavior, regulate the dynamic of handling conflict with your partner, and might even help you make a conscious effort to change your behavior when necessary to transform the dynamic of the relationship.

### Jimmy and Angie

Let's look at Jimmy and Angie as an example. They were fighting; Angie (a Charger) was yelling, and Jimmy literally walked out the door (exhibiting the behavior of a Runner). Oftentimes as a confronter, you want to stop the other person from running, but if Angie had stopped Jimmy from walking out the door, things could have gotten worse. Perhaps it was a fluke that she didn't stop him; he slipped out without her knowledge. Or maybe she let him go because he was despondent. Whether Jimmy was a Runner or just someone who was able to recognize the counter-productiveness of the engagement, he disentangled himself, and in doing so, created space, which Angie allowed for.

So you see, while we tend to act on our most prominent tendency when we're emotionally charged, we're not stuck with one behavior or another. We can move along and operate on a spectrum of traits. Jimmy and Angie eventually came together to talk, but this is not always the case. When you have a fight and are not able to talk it through constructively, it's important to take a break. When we're upset, it may take up to twenty minutes for the body to slow itself down to a calm level. Be sure to set a time to revisit the discussion. Communicate your needs, inform your partner when you intend to come back and resolve the issue, and keep your word. This way, you're not running away from addressing the issue and are able to have a productive and constructive conversation at a later time, when you are both calmer.

That's an important aspect that you need to remember when fighting. You need to turn towards each other, not against one another or away from each other, particularly when it comes to affection. It's easy to withhold affection in anger, but until you're able to communicate and have it resolved, you still need to let each other know that you still love and care for one another. Do *not* withhold affection. Jimmy and Angie had many fights and conflicts throughout their relationship that they tried to resolve through trial and error. It has been said, "A wise man learns from his mistakes, but a wiser man learns from the mistakes of others." You don't necessarily have to repeat their mistakes, but you might be able to learn from their successes.

## What Helped Jimmy and Angie Have a Life of Happy Marriage?

Put simply, the longevity and happiness of Jimmy and Angie's marriage was a result of their commitment to work on their issues together. By living according to the rule of not letting the sun set on your anger, they consciously did not let their issues and anger build up over time. Nothing feels worse than lying three feet away from you partner in bed and feeling thousands of miles apart. The cold and distance you feel when your partner is stonewalling you or shutting you out is detrimental to the soul of the relationship.

Remember that arguments in a relationship are basically a shout-out to your partner that you have something important to say. It's not the nature of the conflict that matters; it's how things are managed that predicts the success or failure of the relationship. Jimmy and Angie were willing to change their unhealthy behaviors to create a positive outcome for their relationship. We each have to make conscious choices every day, whether to build each other up and strengthen our relationship, or tear it down.

According to Gottman, effectively managing conflicts requires you to identify and fight the "Four Horsemen" of conflict whenever they appear. He believes that if you're not able to effectively manage these harbingers of relationship trouble, it will be extremely difficult to resolve your issues.

## THE FOUR HORSEMEN

### The First Horseman: Criticism

This Horseman attacks the character of another person. An example of criticism is, "What's wrong with you? I can't believe you left the toilet seat up again." As you can see, it starts harshly. The antidote for criticism is to *complain without blame*. You need to focus on a specific behavior instead of the person as a whole. For example: "I feel frustrated when I see you leave the seat up. Could you please put it back down after you use it?" Again, use "I" statements and focus on expressing your feelings, followed by a request for a solution.

### The Second Horseman: Defensiveness

Defensiveness serves as self-protection in the form of righteous indignation or innocent victimhood to ward off a perceived attack. Many people become defensive when they are criticized, but the problem is that being defensive never helps to solve the problem at hand. It's just another way of blaming your partner. You're saying that the problem isn't me, it's you. As a result, the problem is not resolved, and the conflict escalates further.

How many times have you gotten a response similar to the following statement in an argument? "It's not my fault that we're always late; you were the one who took an hour to get ready;" or, "I wouldn't be doing this if you didn't push me." To conquer this Horseman, what you can do is to accept your part of the problem. You don't have to take responsibility for the whole thing, but you do need to recognize how you play a role in the situation and verbalize it, such as, "Well, part of this is my problem; I do need to be more conscientious of time."

### The Third Horseman: Stonewalling

Stonewalling is one possible result after a listener withdraws from an interaction. If the other person persists in the discussion, the person who withdrew will either explode at them or else refuse to acknowledge them, otherwise known as stonewalling. Neither behavior is helpful in moving forward constructively. When you feel this way, it's important to let your partner know that you're feeling flooded and need a break. While on break, you can physiologically self-soothe with activities such as deep breathing, meditating, listening to music, or exercising. And then return to your discussion.

### The Fourth Horseman: Contempt

It's crucial to avoid thoughts of righteous indignation or victimization, such as, "I don't have to take this anymore," or, "Why is she always picking on me?" The other side of feeling victimized is *contempt*. *Contempt* involves using superiority statements that are often expressed through sarcasm, cynicism, eye rolling, sneering, mockery, hostile humor, and name-calling. According to Gottman, contempt is the greatest predictor of divorce and must be eliminated. Let me stress that: contempt is a great predictor of a broken marriage and should generally be avoided (though this is not necessarily *always* the case).

### Jon and Maria

Jon and Maria are a perfect example of how a marriage can survive contempt when the couple is on the same wavelength. They didn't come to me because of marital issues; rather, Maria had been feeling blue since her youngest child had left the nest. Maria's identity as an adult was based on her being a wife and mother. She worked part-time on and off, but her work is not something she really counts as a life achievement. It's not easy for her now that all her children are off on their own and away from home.

What I enjoyed most was how Jon and Maria acted as husband and wife. They have absolutely no filters with each other, even in my office. Most couples tend to refrain from yelling or cursing in front of me, but not Jon and Maria. In one of the sessions, we were discussing what Maria could do with her time to help her move forward more easily.

Jon suggested, "Maybe you could start gardening and see how good you are at nurturing plants."

"Fuck you!" Maria snapped.

I had my hand up immediately, signaling for a stop, as this typically led nowhere but to Unpleasantville. But before I could get a word out, Maria continued, "You're just being a dick. You know how terrible I am at it."

To be honest, I was nervous, since this was only their first session with me. But to my surprise, Jon replied with a smirk on his face, "And you're with me, so what does it make you?"

To which Maria responded, "You're an asshole," and Jon, smiling, said, "I know."

As a psychologist practicing for over a decade, I can't say I see this behavior often. Logically, I had to further explore that little exchange they had just had. I found out that it's not abnormal for them to bicker and banter in this way; it's actually one of their ways to make light of things. It serves as a reminder to them to not take things too seriously. The exchange I'd witnessed was Jon's way of pointing out how Maria was getting intense. Maria was in turn able to acknowledge her shortcomings while calling Jon names. They knew exactly what they were doing, and their partner understood; it's their own secret code. Again, this is not for everyone. The key is understanding each other's intentions and communication.

## EXERCISE: SELF-REFLECTION

It's natural to have conflicts in a relationship. What you do about these conflicts—how you handle them—is what matters. You can turn your conflict and confusion into clarity and connection, depending on how you approach them.

**One simple exercise I have clients do when they find themselves in a destructive argument to help them take a break and be reflective of their own behavior is:**

1. Pause, with the intention to come back within a short period of time.

2. Individually pick a corner of the house, sit, examine the situation, and fill out the form below.

3. Resume for a healthy discussion in a mutually agreed-upon place.

| | ME | MY PARTNER (PERCEIVED) |
|---|---|---|
| **Exhibiting emotion** | i.e. angry and hurt | i.e. angry |
| **Intention** | i.e. to let my partner know I need help with chores | i.e. he just wants to shut me down |
| **What was done correctly** | i.e. I asked in a normal tone when brought up initially | i.e. he didn't yell |
| **What needs to be improve** | i.e. I could remain calm to explain to him what I need | i.e. he attentively listens to what I had to say instead of making excuses |
| **What I really want from this** | i.e. my partner to take the trash out every Sunday | i.e. I think he just wants me to take care of all the chores |

It's essential for you to work together, not against one another, for the success of the relationship. Learning effective communication styles and listening skills can help you to have a softer start to your dialogue and to be understood. Identifying your way of handling conflicts and working together with your partner to avoid *any* Horsemen will help you resolve your issues and feel more respected and loved. And more importantly, learn to verbally express your feelings rather than acting on them. Remember, "You catch more flies with honey than you do with vinegar," so keep the sweet, positive comments and behavior to the maximum on a daily basis. In order for a couple to have a happy relationship, the ratio of positive to negative interactions needs to be 20 to 1. Your emotional bank account needs to have consistent deposits by both parties with a sufficient amount of funds, so that when you need to make withdrawals, the balance doesn't go into the negative. And when negative interactions arise, it doesn't matter what your personality or tendencies were in dealing with conflicts in the past; you can always learn to change them to make them better and more constructive.

In short? Fights happen in relationships. When there's a fight, it's important to keep in mind that you don't fight to win; you fight for the betterment of your relationship. Don't go in with swords drawn and shields up; go in with a gentle voice and an open heart. That's how you learn more about each other and make improvements in your relationship. That's how you build and maintain a happy, passionate marriage.

[ 9 ]

# Exciting Sex

Sex is always about emotions. Good sex is
about free emotions; bad sex is about blocked
emotions ... Sex is an emotion in motion.

—Deepak Chopra

Sex. Everyone is doing it, but no one is talking about it. In
fact, it's embarrassing to talk about. But we can't talk about relationships without including sex.

It's a fascinating topic that most of us are curious about, but
it also seems to be taboo to have an open discussion about sex.
There's an unspoken element of guilt and shame when it comes
to sex, and we end up shaming it instead of embracing it as a
beautiful act of connection.

Sex is the most physical act of intimacy two persons can share
with one another. It's an expression of love—which may be

old-fashioned of me to think, especially in our hookup culture. When we can't have love, we all too often settle for lust. Modern culture has turned sex into cheap, fifteen-minute thrills.

In this discussion, I want to take you beyond the physical pleasure of sex to talk about the psychological and emotional stimulation that comes from this most beautiful and basic of acts.

## ARE YOU DATING OR "DUCKING"?

Dating seems to have a new meaning, going by what my young single adult clients have told me. "You can have sex without dating," they explain, "but you can't date without having sex." Back in the old days, courtship was about truly getting to know the other person. However, nowadays it seems that dating and sex are synonymous, as is the phrase is "hang out and hook up."

The trouble is that sex can complicate and convolute a budding romance. We know oxytocin, the "love chemical" which gives you feelings of attachment, is released after sex. Hence, when sex happens too early in a dating scene, it can give a false sense of closeness, one which is neither substantial nor sustainable if there is no other foundation.

When you eliminate sex in the beginning of a new romance, you can quickly discern the intentions of the other person. You also have more clarity on forming the other types of substantial intimacy that build a strong foundation for a healthy relationship. On top of that, it also helps you to distinguish the difference between lust and love. Lust is like a mushroom that quickly sprouts up but also quickly dies away, whereas love is like an oak tree that takes years to take root and grow, but is strong enough to weather any storm.

All too frequently, I have heard complaints from both genders of the shortcomings of "meaningless" sex. "It gets old," they say.

I'm sure it does; in order to make sex more meaningful, other form of intimacies need to form before physical intimacy occurs. It's best not to be "ducking in dating," I tell my clients. No-strings-attached one-night stands or casual sex may seem appealing, but sex only gets better when you feel safe and secure. It takes you to a whole different level of pleasantry and intimacy.

## What Kind of Song Do You Want to Write?

Sex is one of the top three topics couples come into counseling for. Some couples are still in their honeymoon stage, others are lifelong partners, but the sex issues are similar. Some of the common statements I have heard are "Our sex life isn't that great," "We don't have sex anymore," "He asks for too much," "She wants too little," "He wants it vanilla," and "She wants kinky." Once in a while, I even hear the shocked response of, "You want what?!"

One time, a male client said to me, "I love my wife, but after fifteen years with her, it's like having chicken every day for fifteen years. Don't get me wrong, I love chicken, but sometimes I want beef, pork, and other stuff, too, you know?"

I laughed and said that perhaps he needed to prepare his chicken differently each day, but I knew exactly what he was talking about. Generally, we tend to seek out new and novel experiences for excitement. After years of having the same sex with the same partner, things can become stale and stagnant. It happens in every relationship until you work with each other to find a deeper connection.

It's important for you to be creative, and equally important to have an honest conversation with each other. An unsatisfying sex life is one of the top reasons for infidelity. While it is in no way a license to cheat, often people step out of a committed monogamous relationship because of unfulfilled needs. Thankfully, unsatisfying sex is a solvable one. A sex life that once was hot can often be easily revived with a little information and a willingness on both parts to experiment.

But what about the couples who have just gotten together? What could possibly stop them from having a steamy sex life?

We tend to want and crave what is not there, but once we have it, we become satisfied and lose the sense of urgency that comes with the original craving. We tend to enjoy novel experiences, but the other side of novelty is mastery. It can take a lifetime to master techniques, especially when it comes to sex. I'm not talking about the mechanics of it; try to think of love as a song and lovemaking as an instrument. When you play an instrument, you know that you can get away with playing the basic chords. On a guitar, you can basically write a song knowing only three chords. In the same way, it is fairly easy to have sex from a mechanical standpoint. But oftentimes, the songs that touch the soul take more than three chords to fully convey its beautiful melody.

What kind of a song do you want to create?

## ARE YOU HAVING SEX?

*Tim and Jessica*

Before mastering any sexual techniques, let's first start with the question, "Are you actively having sex? Or is it the first thing to go in your relationship when you're busy?"

In the first couple of years, sex was hot and heavy for Tim and Jessica. They couldn't keep their hands off of each other. But now, sex has become a form of maintenance for them.

"We're like this old, boring couple," said Jessica.

"We used to sneak into public bathrooms and did it in all these crazy places," Tim added.

"He's my best friend," Jessica said.

"And she's mine," Tim continued. "Everything in our lives is great. We work together seamlessly as a team. Except we don't really have sex anymore."

It's their fifth year together. Somewhere along the way, Tim and Jessica forgot what it's like to want each other. They treat each other like an old Christmas toy; they were really excited about getting it, played with it for a while, and then got bored with it.

They described their lives as busy professionals with long hours. They both are exhausted at the end of the day. "We get home, cook, have our meals, and maybe sit down with a drink or two to unwind, and before you know it, it's time to get ready for bed. Trying to get some sleep in sounds more appealing than trying to have sex when you know that you have to wake up early in the morning and do it all over again," Jessica confessed.

### Joanna and Ben

This is a typical problem for a lot of couples. Many couples find themselves without enough time for sex.

Joanna is a stay-at-home mom who doesn't have the same problem as Jessica, but the words her husband Ben utters are no different: they don't have enough sex. Joanna is taking care of a five-year-old son, a three-year-old daughter, and a nine-month-old baby.

"I love my kids, and I wouldn't trade them for anything in the world, but I feel like I had it easier when I was working ten hours a day," Joanna confessed, tearing up. "Now, I feel like I'm working around the clock nonstop without pay. After feedings, diaper changes, cooking, cleaning, and giving everything I have to the kids, I don't feel like doing any more giving. I know he has needs and I shouldn't deprive him, but I can only give so much, you know."

The circumstances may be different, but the issue remains. Their schedules don't have room for sex. Or to be more accurate, they don't have sex included in their schedules. They make time for what they deem are the important activities, but when it comes to sex, they leave it to chance.

Early in the relationship, these chances come more often. However, over the years, many relationships suffer as sex frequency inevitably wanes. To bring the spice back into a relationship, we have to start at the foundation by creating a stable schedule for sex.

No couple is ever thrilled at the idea of scheduling their sex time. It sounds strange to mark your calendar with "Sex on Tuesday, 8:30 PM." The unanimous protest I often hear is that sex should be spontaneous, but the reality is that it has never truly been spontaneous. When you are new to a relationship, you anticipate, think about, and plan for sex. Sex was a seed that you wanted to plant so that it would grow, and you made plans accordingly to create the mood. It's easy to get caught up with the busyness of life, but you need to make time to reignite the passion and connection you once had. When you leave things up to spontaneity, you're relying on the alignment of pure physical urges that both of you have in that moment, and that rarely happens. That's when you hear comments such as, "I don't feel good" or "I have a headache." Sex is an important aspect of your relationship; don't leave it to chance, make a choice to have it. Remember, the more sex you have, the more oxytocin—love chemical—will be released in your brain, which makes you feel happier and closer together, which, in turn, creates a new dynamic where you naturally want to have more sex.

## WHAT IF IT'S SOMETHING DEEPER?

*Eliot*

Eliot had found himself stuck in a vicious cycle: he keeps dating women who are not available. When he finds a woman that he is able to talk to and open up to emotionally, he finds they have no physical chemistry, and their sex is nonexistent. However, when he finds himself wanting to get physically intimate and have incredible sex, he can't open up emotionally, or he doesn't see a future with the woman.

Eliot is avoiding intimacy. As long as he's dating women who are not available, then no true intimacy will form, and he won't get hurt by being vulnerable. Twice, he has found himself able to connect intellectually, emotionally, physically, and spiritually *and* could see a future with the person ... but one was in a committed relationship and the other was married.

Sex is not just sex. Unless there is a medical issue, most sex issues are psychological in origin. We have established that Eliot has a fear of intimacy due to his attachment issues, so as long as there is a barrier of any kind, it will keep him from moving forward, which means he won't be completely invested in a relationship. That's something he is not ready for.

But what about the two women in committed relationships who had an affair with Eliot? Oftentimes, people think affairs are about sex, but it is more than that. Affairs are often the result of a fear of vulnerability and intimacy. It's a fear of rejection. And sometimes, it's a loss of connection that needs rebuilding.

*Nolan*

Nolan has a perfect marriage and a beautiful family. There's just one problem: "The sex sucks. It's so boring that I fall asleep," he tells me.

Nolan has been married for seven years and has been cheating on his wife for six. He came in because he wanted to figure out "what's wrong with him."

"I don't *like* cheating on my wife. She is a great wife, the mother of my children, but I just can't help it. I have a list of girls that I cycle through. I don't just get with one girl. That's bad."

"How often do you have sex with your wife?" I asked.

"Maybe once a week. Twice, when we drink on the weekends. It's better when we're drunk."

"How often do you go outside of your marriage?"

"Two or three times a week. Sometimes once a week if I'm too busy."

"Do you have sex under the influence with others, too?"

"No, I don't need to."

"What makes you need it to improve things with your wife?"

"I don't know. I guess I don't have to worry."

"Worry about what?"

"I can do whatever I want with other women, but I can't do those things to my wife."

Nolan gets turned on by certain stimuli and sexual acts. It doesn't excite him to have sex in the missionary position, but that's all he and his wife do—vanilla sex. He's not comfortable talking about sex with his wife. His perception is that anything besides missionary is "dirty," and you can't talk about it intelligently. Nolan needed to learn that it's normal to talk about sex in colorful language. So long as he's not comfortable talking about it, he won't be able to bring it up with his wife.

We needed to help him normalize sex and his desire. He was embarrassed to finally admit that the most adventurous sexual act with his wife was doggy style, which only occurs when they're drunk. But that's as far as they would go, because what he enjoys is "not acceptable in a marriage." He thinks it's lewd and indecent. To use his exact words: "I can't treat my wife like a whore." When he's with other women, he doesn't have to worry about degrading them, whereas his wife, the mother of his children, deserves respect. Logically, it doesn't make much sense, but it is the perfect solution to Nolan. He believes that he remains respectful of his wife in the bedroom, and because he doesn't develop any emotional attachments by rotating women, then what he is doing is "acceptable."

We first examined his thought process. What Nolan failed to realize is that each time he steps out of his marriage, he is chipping away at it. He's making the foundation less and less stable. We also addressed his distorted perception of sex, sexual positions, and techniques. My hope was to get him to understand that these things don't define who he is as a person; rather, it is just one of his preferences for sexual gratification and enjoyment. Nor does it say who his wife is as a person. It's just like some of us find pleasure in a chocolate-dipped strawberry, whereas others would prefer a bite of vanilla ice cream.

After weeks and weeks of talking, he came to accept what he likes and that there's no shame in it. He needed to bring his wife into his world and share this intimate part of himself with her. His wife was delighted with the idea of spicing up their bedroom life. What he once thought was forbidden and had to be kept as a dirty little secret was now shared and enjoyed by both.

As far as his long-term affairs with multiple women, we spent a good amount of time talking about what is best for him and his marriage. He decided that it was best not to tell his wife. He believes that he should tell her only if he wanted a divorce, and he doesn't want that. He believes that his wife must have had some sense of when it was happening. She didn't say anything, perhaps because she didn't want to believe it or to protect her dignity. He thinks that it would destroy her and taint the relationship moving forward.

Is it better to keep an affair quiet if you are never going to do it again? That depends on who you ask and what you believe. There's no "one size fits all" when it comes to relationships, even though we have thoroughly discussed that intimacy is formed and deepened with vulnerability.

### Jack and Diane

Jack and Diane may be one of the few exceptional couples who were able to rebuild their relationship after an affair. Oftentimes, we believe that an affair ends a marriage, but not for these two.

Diane and Jack were together for seven years before they decided to tie the knot. In those seven years, they were dating for four years and had a long engagement. It took them a long time to make that final commitment because Diane wanted to make sure that she was making the right decision. She has always had a fear of making a lifelong commitment, as she believes that marriage is forever.

The story she relayed seems straight out of a movie. Diane ran into her ex-lover on a business trip. "I didn't think anything would happen; I was holding my ground," she insists. "I was not going to do my husband wrong, you know. I love him. But the weird thing is it seemed like no time had passed since I last saw him. It felt exactly as it was twelve years ago."

Diane described her relationship with her ex as tumultuously passionate. They were like magnets to each other. But time and time again, for one reason or another, they cut each other off, only to eventually come back together again.

"It was so bad that I knew it would never work. But I don't quite understand what it is that gets ahold of me. I literally get stupid when I'm with him. I'm an intelligent woman, and I can't seem to form a coherent sentence to talk to him. He makes me anxious, and I don't like it. I get weak in the knees and I melt at his touch."

"What happened between you two when you ran into him?" I asked.

"We had a couple of drinks. We talked and caught up on our lives. I don't know how it happened, but then he started touching my hands, and we ended up kissing. It was electrifying." She paused with both of her hands cupping her face and let out a deep breath. "We fooled around," she continued. "The thing is that it felt so natural. I completely let myself go as he took me to places that I wouldn't even feel comfortable doing with my husband."

"Did you have sex with him?"

"No, not intercourse, but other stuff and still ..."

We took the time to process her feelings about John, the man from her past, her actions and their functions, her marriage, and ultimately, her feelings toward Jack, her husband. She said that she loved Jack, but she was confused because she didn't feel guilty about what she did. We further explored her perception of Jack and the ex-lover. When I asked her about the last time she had really looked at Jack, she was baffled by the question.

"What do you mean?" she asked.

"When was the last time you looked at him not as Jack, *your* husband, but Jack as a *man* who's not within your reach?"

"I don't know. He's my *husband*; he's always within my reach."

"Are you certain that he's *always* yours?"

"Probably not after what I did."

Diane had believed for the longest time that Jack was not going anywhere. He was hers to keep and access whenever she wanted. It was too easy and too convenient. He became another routine in her life. She doesn't see him as a man who is coveted by many other women. She sees him as a man in her pocket. She had stopped seeing him as a man who she once coveted. Her marriage started to get stale and stagnant, whereas with John, things were exciting and "electrifying." Jack didn't make her earn his attention and affection, hence she didn't appreciate him.

I don't think things really registered for Diane until she seriously thought about telling him the truth. She realized then that she may actually lose him, and came to the conclusion that asking for a divorce would be the easier thing to do, as it would help her feel more in control. Telling Jack what had happened, on the other hand, would be the most vulnerable thing she could do; she'd be putting herself at his mercy. With that realization, Diane decided to tell Jack, as they have always valued honesty in their relationship. They respect one another enough not to make unilateral decision regarding their relationship. It's a fundamental belief that they share, and it didn't matter how hurtful the truth might be.

It was the risk of losing that made her appreciate the staying. For the first time in their relationship, Diane was genuinely afraid of losing Jack. She realized that she had taken him for granted; that just because he is her husband doesn't mean he will always be hers.

Diane was relieved and happy when they decided they'd stay together and work through their issues. Though she will need to earn Jack's trust again, she was surprised to find out that her husband thought her courageous for coming forward. Knowing the truth can help them to reevaluate their relationship—determine what is missing—so they can make it better.

We continued to work on Diana's attachment style and to help her realize that she is loved and worthy of love. She doesn't need to sabotage her relationship or keep testing her husband. He loves her, unconditionally. I also had them implement a little bedroom exercise (see below) to help them reconnect with each other.

*Bedroom Connection*

> **Set aside 5 uninterrupted minutes of your time for this exercise to reconnect with your partner:**
>
> 1. Set your alarm for one minute. During this minute, you and your partner will sit in bed facing each other, holding hands and simply gazing into each other's eyes without talking.
>
> 2. Tell your partner the feelings and appreciation you have for him or her (reserve one minute for each person).
>
> 3. Reserve an additional minute for each partner to express what you'd like your partner to do sexually with you.

Diane reported back after six months that the dynamic of their relationship had changed. They're much happier, and she noticed she was much more patient and affectionate toward Jack. She is pleased with the outcome and her decision-making. She believes that if she had kept things secret, it would have been cancerous to their relationship, and it might have allowed her to continue to behave badly knowing that she had gotten away with it.

Sex is a simple act that has many implications and complications. In Jack and Diane's case, they needed to rebuild trust after a sexual dilemma. But sometimes, it takes sex to know how much you trust a person.

*Benjamin and Edith*

Benjamin considers himself a straight-laced man. He abides by the rules and doesn't deviate from the norm. His number one fear growing up, and to this day, is getting into trouble. He's afraid of the consequences that he would have to face, and the idea that he has done something wrong or possibly hurt some-one is terrifying.

Benjamin has been a great source of support for his long-term partner—financially and emotionally. But when it comes to sex, that's a different story.

"I'm telling you, the things Edith wants me to do to her make no sense to me. I'm having a hard time. But she also keeps turn-ing me down when I initiate. I'm tired of doing that, and we haven't really had sex since last summer."

"What is it that Edith asked you to do?"

"She wants me to 'take her.' She wants me to be more aggres-sive with her, pull her hair, slap her, and stuff. Sounds like abuse to me. And the thing is that she told me she was sexually abused when she was younger. That's just wrong, you know. I don't want to abuse her when she has already been hurt."

Edith admitted it didn't much make sense to her, either. She didn't understand why she would want to subject herself to that stuff, but she can't deny that it's a personal turn-on for her.

"Is that how you typically want to engage sexually?"

"No. I'm usually opposite to that. It takes a long time for me to open up sexually. I'm quite shy in bed, actually."

Their sexual relationship had gradually decreased over the years. Edith didn't find it satisfactory, but she didn't know how to communicate that to Ben. One day, she blurted it out to Ben in an argument. Ben didn't know how to take it or what to do with it. They'd never discussed it again. Ben went back to his old way of initiating sex by offering to give her massages and hoping that would get her into the mood. When that didn't work, he was left feeling frustrated and defeated, and she was left feeling disappointed and unsatisfied.

We looked into Benjamin's uncomfortable feelings with her request and his need to protect her. We also looked into Edith's sexual history and desires. We needed to figure out how they both could get their needs met.

Edith's sexual abuse had left her feeling violated and not in control. Naturally, it seemed counterintuitive when she asked Ben to take control of her sexually; it just seemed like a torturous reenactment of her trauma. What they didn't realize was that on an unconscious level, Edith knew that she remained in control; unlike her trauma, with Benjamin, she can stop anytime she chooses. Therefore, allowing herself to lose control is an indication of the trust she has for Benjamin. In this way, she is actually liberated by the activity, as she's regaining control of herself and her relationship through sex.

As for Benjamin, once he realized that he was not hurting her or doing the wrong thing, he was open to the idea, especially when he knew he wouldn't get rejected. What's more important is that this really helped get him out of his shell. It helped him to learn to be more assertive and confident, areas he needed to improve in his own life. As they continue to communicate their fantasies and better execute their sexual desires, they increase the depth of their sexual intimacy with one another.

As Benjamin and Edith did, many couples come to learn that sex is beautiful, an act which plays an intricate part in a relationship. It doesn't have to be a taboo, especially as it is another avenue that can deepen the intimacy of our relationships. When we step outside of our relationship, physically or emotionally, we're weakening it. But when we openly communicate to our partners what we like and don't like, we're strengthening ours by allowing ourselves to be a bit more vulnerable.

The other side of this coin is that you open yourself to all-new experiences, learning how loving and attentive your partner can be by honoring your needs. That is how intimacy is built. Furthermore, you get to have a more satisfying sex life.

Just remember that there's no "one size fits all" when it comes to sex. Our bodies respond differently to stimuli in ways colored by our own emotional experiences. When we fail to communicate what we like and how we like it, we're leaving our partner to stumble in the dark, hoping to hit the right target.

Learning to recognize the enchanting melody of sex can rock your world!

# [ 10 ]

# *Money Matters*

So it's not gonna be easy. It's going to be really
hard; we're gonna have to work at this every
day, but I want to do that because I want you. I
want all of you, forever, every day. You and me
... every day

– Nicholas Sparks, *The Notebook*

## Money Can't Buy Happiness, But...

Money plays a crucial role in a relationship. We all need to acknowledge this fact in order for us to talk openly about it. And you can't deny that it is problematic for a relationship when you're struggling financially. You can have a whole lot of love, but having very little money will put a strain on your relationship. It's not romantic, but it *is* reality. Money, or the lack thereof, can create a number of issues for many couples, especially when you don't know how to deal with them.

Like sex, money is another topic that many couples steer clear of talking about. Of course, that doesn't stop them from complaining about it to the point that it can potentially lead to divorce—and unfortunately does for many couples. So, let's avoid that by being more proactive with money matters early on in a relationship.

A friend of mine and I were talking about his single status one day. Even though he's very successful financially, he wants the women he dates to be financially independent. He doesn't need her to work, but he sees it as a trait of a strong woman that she has a life of her own doing what she wants.

"I just hate that when some girls find out about my success, they want to quit their jobs and have me take care of them. It's fine if we were married and we had kids that she needs to take care of, but that's not yet the case."

It made me laugh, but I could understand how he feels.

*Betty*

Betty is a client of mine in her early fifties who is still looking for someone who will marry and take care of her. Tired of being a waitress, she wants nothing less than the *Pretty Woman* fairytale. She only dates wealthy men and wants to live the life of jet-setting and fine dining.

The interesting fact is that she willingly spends hundreds of dollars to visit the man in his hometown, where he takes her out to five-star restaurants to wine and dine her for the evening. He then takes her back to his place, or sometimes her hotel room. But the money she spends on traveling to visit him and on hotels is enough to treat herself to lavish experiences she craves. She has been doing this for thirty years and has yet to find a man who will marry her. She said she's come close a couple of times, with men who told her that they loved her, who wanted to take her on trips and marry her, but it never happened.

When we talked about her relationship and her expectations, Betty made it clear that the man must bring finances to the table.

"And what do you bring to the table, if I may ask?" I asked.

"Sex," she replied with absolute conviction.

She truly believes that what she needs to bring to the relationship is sex. I had to point out the harsh truth that the men she was dating didn't have to marry her to have sex with her. It might even be a lot cheaper for them to just sample what she (and others) had to offer.

Money problems typically don't happen early on in a relationship. In the beginning, most couples are financially independent from one another. Neither of you have any unrealistic expectations about money; instead, you have a greater appreciation for when and how it is spent on each other. Therefore, most lovers do not talk about money until they merge their lives and finances together.

That's a mistake. It is important to learn early on about your potential partner's attitude toward money. You shouldn't wait until your life is entwined to find out your partner's spending habits. I do believe it's worse not knowing how to manage your money compared to not having it. When you don't have money, you can work to earn it. But if you don't know how to manage your money, it will develop legs and walk right out of your bank account. This is the reason why some lottery winners stay broke even after winning millions of dollars. They blow through it like it will never run out.

Even a few lighthearted questions can provide serious insight into a person's ability to earn and spend money. On your first date, feel free to ask hypothetical questions such as, "What would you do if you won a fortune?" This simple question can reveal how money conscious and responsible a person is. If the answer revolves around living it up like a king with no thoughts of saving, investing, or future retirement concerns, then generally speaking, the person has poor money management skills. Some other questions you might also ask are: "Are you good at saving money?" "What would you do if you were the richest person in the world?" "Do you ever give money to charity?" "When was the last time you were broke?" "What do you think of credit cards?" "How would you blow $5,000 in a weekend?", and so on.

Once you're in a committed relationship and thinking of building a life together, it is even more important for you to have an in-depth financial discussion. Most couples need to discuss what financial experts refer to as the "double Os"—what you owe and what you own. The sooner you figure it out, the more prepared you'll be for your future. There will also be fewer surprises when you're ready to build your life together.

### Samantha and Brian

Samantha and Brian were recently married, and neither expected to start building their life together on a foundation of debts. Samantha and Brian had agreed to put their honeymoon expenses on a credit card that they would work to pay off later. However, that was not the only credit card debt they had. They both had more than one credit card and owed thousands of dollars on each card. Samantha wants to be debt-free as soon as possible so they could possibly buy a house, and is frustrated that Brian is worse than she is when it comes to money management.

"I know I splurge and buy myself a $300 purse sometimes, but I make sure that my bill is taken care of first. I don't usually buy anything; this shirt that I'm wearing is two years old and I bought it for like $15. I know I shouldn't say anything because he can splurge every now and then, too, but I want us to pay off our debts, save money, and maybe buy a place eventually," Samantha said, voicing her frustration.

"I know I'm not that great at saving money, but I hate how she thinks the way she spends money is correct. But when it comes to me, what I think is important, she thinks can wait," Brian argued.

Samantha jumped back in. "Let me give you an example. We have a hand-me-down couch from my parents. It's nothing fancy, but it's fine. It has some stains on it, since we have two dogs and they love to jump on it, which we're okay with. But they drool. So instead of maybe just cleaning up the stain or getting some sort of cover-up, Brian went out and just bought a new couch. At the end of the month, when I asked him for his half of the bill, he didn't have enough to give me. I had to cover for him. I know there are times when he takes me out to dinner because he has just gotten paid, and I appreciate that—a lot. It's really sweet of him to want to treat me to something nice. But it's frustrating that I have to keep covering for his share of the bills. I would prefer he kept the money and help me take care of the bills rather than take me out. Just like we didn't really need to buy that couch at that time."

It is difficult to talk about money without tripping over the emotions behind it. A lot of times, it touches the sensitive area of personal adequacy (or lack thereof). We came to understand that Brian didn't have much growing up; it was always about trying to make ends meet in his family. His mom was a nanny for the neighborhood kids while also taking care of him and his siblings. His father was a truck driver who was rarely home. When he *was* home, it was usually after he had just been paid, and he spoiled the whole family. He'd take them out to a nice dinner or get something for the house. Going shopping and having dinner out with his family are his happy memories.

Brian tries to recreate those happy memories with Samantha. It makes him feel like a man who can treat his wife to a nice evening. He believes that everything will work out in the end, and doesn't think about Samantha's perspective. She has to work extra shifts to pick up extra money to cover his share of the bills, but he thinks everything is fine as he pays Samantha back with his next paycheck.

We looked into the dynamics of their relationship and their different attitudes toward money. We focused on what Brian wants, and determined that he *does* share Samantha's goals—he wants to live comfortably, have enough to splurge, have a house, and build a family. What he doesn't want is to worry about using up all of his paycheck for bills or paying back Samantha. In particular, he doesn't want his wife telling him how to spend his money.

After we established what Brian wanted, he's become more motivated to make changes. He no longer feels like he has to do it for Samantha; he's doing it for himself. We discussed choices and financial management options that make the most sense for the couple. They decided that having three bank accounts was best in their situation. They both agree to put ninety percent of their income into the joint account to take care of shared responsibilities and living expenses. The rest will go into their individual accounts for discretionary use. Otherwise, a discussion is necessary before a decision is made on how to spend joint money. They also sat down with a financial advisor, who helped them go over all of their debts and goals so they can efficiently allocate their funds.

I'm certain that Samantha and Brian's finances will be much

smoother down the line. More importantly, they've avoided the unnecessary resentment over money that was building up in their relationship.

Resentment can also develop when there's a significant difference in income levels, particularly when the woman makes more money compared to her partner in a heterosexual relationship. The number of primary women breadwinners is on the rise as women begin taking advantage of the opportunities for higher education and better jobs. However, having a female breadwinner can stir up trouble in marriages, perhaps because our collective unconscious sees men as providers and women as nurturers. When the roles are reversed, some men are not able to deal with it gracefully and feel emasculated.

### Adam and Amy

Adam has been a stay-at-home dad for twenty years, ever since his daughter was born. It made more sense for Adam to stay at home, since his wife Amy was bringing home a bigger paycheck. Her work is also more stable than Adam's, who works as a freelance musician.

However, as the years went by, most of their friends who were stay-at-home moms and dads went back to work after their kids started school. Yet Adam still maintains his stay-at-home status, even after their daughter has been out of the house at college for two years.

Amy and Adam came into therapy because they were struggling with their marriage. What bothers Amy is that she feels like Adam's not trying. "He was really good with the saxophone, but he's not playing anymore," she explains. "He spends all day at home fixing computers, but it's not like he's making much with it. And if he gets paid, do you know what he does? He goes to the grocery store and stocks up our refrigerator, but we end up throwing most of it out. I usually won't eat the stuff he buys, since it's high in fat and unhealthy."

As it turns out, Adam is a very laid-back man. From the beginning of their relationship, Amy was always the one behind the wheel. Whenever Adam failed to meet the mark, Amy anxiously took over. After Adam missed a few payments on their bills, Amy took over their finances. In fact, she's taken over most of the tasks around the house. It used to help her feel good, because she felt she was playing a crucial role in the family, but it's begun to catch up to her.

There is a harsh reality that Amy needs to face. She must acknowledge her part in this codependent relationship. She has "created a monster" without realizing it. She wanted to feel important, so she took on a role that was unintentionally created for her. Everyone in the family depends on her for finances and the other services she provides. She, in turn, gets fed emotionally through their dependency. To help Amy and Adam reestablish their relationship and come to a healthier financial arrangement, Amy needed to first step out of the role she's been playing and learn that she is important without creating dependency for her family.

As for the finances, we started out small to ease her anxiety. (We also needed to start out small to set Adam up for success before we tackled bigger challenges.) We discussed better options to put Adam's money to use. Since Adam is a bit messy and doesn't seem to feel the need to clean up after himself after making a mess, and Amy hates coming home to see dirty dishes on the counter, it was agreed that they would get a housekeeper once a week, and that Adam would take care of the cost.

As for Amy, she needs to learn to recognize Adam's different contributions. While he's not contributing exactly what she wants, that doesn't mean his contribution is worth less in value.

He has certainly helped her navigate the technology world with her computer and tablet, which she enjoys every day.

With that said, there are many elements to making sure a household runs smoothly, and no chore takes care of itself. Adam and Amy needed to learn to negotiate household tasks and assign a value system to them. They then divide them up based on their strengths, resulting in great overall equitability in the relationship. While equality in a relationship is often impossible and usually unadvisable, equitability is essential. To explain the difference, equal contribution is saying, "I'll clean 50% of the time and you clean 50% of the time" regardless of whether both do a good job or not. Equitability is saying, "I'm a great cook so I'll cook 90% of the time, and you enjoy cleaning so you do it 90% of the time."

Both partners in a relationship must work together and share the responsibility of keeping the relationship moving. It's also important to be mindful of not overestimating your efforts and undermining those of your partner. I recommend implementing a sort of chores list or tasks table, like the one included in Appendix B of this book.

### Darlene and Edward

Darlene and Edward are another example of a couple where the wife earns more money. The difference between Darlene and Amy is that Darlene doesn't feel that she does most of the work. As a matter of fact, she recognizes that Edward does a lot for the family. In this case, Edward is the one who is resentful. Edward was once a young entrepreneur who was supporting Darlene through medical school, but ever since the economic crash in 2008, he hasn't been able to bounce back to the level where he once was. Initially, he was okay with it, as he thought it was only temporary. But as the years pass, he grows more and more resentful toward his wife. He feels inadequate. His friends, who share the same beliefs he does, also think that the husband should be a provider who is able to take care of his wife. They tell him that Darlene's wearing the pants in the relationship because she makes more money.

Edward and his friends are not alone in their feelings. Many men feel insecure when their wife makes more money, especially if their income alone is not sufficient to provide for the family. The effect on their self-esteem seems lessened if, regardless of how much more their wife makes, their own income alone would be enough to take care of their family. In other words, if the husband can contextualize the wife's larger paycheck as "extra" or "bonus" money, their pride isn't injured. What this really suggests is that our perception and attitude toward money and the power that we allow it to have weighs heavily on our relationships. It's not the amount of money that matters, but whether we feel that we're adequate or not.

When we got to the core of the issue, Edward was afraid that Darlene would look at him as less than a man, or that she would leave him for someone better—to be more accurate, someone more financially successful. Darlene was able to help Edward see that he's not measured by how much he makes in her eyes. She helped him realize that, while she makes more money, he provides so much to their relationship by giving her stability and love, and helping her to feel grounded and wanted, not to mention the contribution he made towards her career early on. She acknowledges that he plays a part in her success.

Edward's self-esteem needed a boost, and we were able to help him recognize his ability and bolster his belief in himself again so that he could focus on himself and be more supportive of his wife's success. Darlene also made it clear to him that it's not a competition, and her success is also his success.

There's an old adage: "Money is the root of all evil." But money is *not* the root of all evil; it is how we look at it and use it that makes a difference. When you have it, money can give you the luxury and freedom to buy entertainment for your relationship. It can also serve as a testimony of how well you work together through your trials and hardships when you don't feel like you have enough. At the end of the day, money is only another aspect of our lives. When we're financially independent and stable, it gives us another sense of security. When we're secure on our own, sharing that security with another makes the feeling even better.

Remember, money provides you another avenue for you to strengthen your relationship. Each time you discuss what makes you feel uncomfortable, you deepen the intimacy you have with your partner. It is necessary for you to prepare and plan your finances as individuals as well as together so you can be twice as strong. Healthy and happy relationships need a strong foundation. I want you to take care of your money matters so it becomes one less source of worry in your relationship. The less worry you have in your relationship, the more you can keep it alive and lively.

# Dynamic Duo

> When we love, we always strive to become better than we are. When we strive to become better than we are, everything around us becomes better, too.
>
> — Paulo Coelho, *The Alchemist*

MY DAYS AT work are always interesting, but some days are more interesting than others. Recently, I had an unusually interesting day where two clients back-to-back discussed the two fundamentally different sides of a relationship.

*Alexia*
Here's a puzzle that most people encounter when dating. Why do people keep going back to or dating someone who treats them like dirt?

My 10 AM appointment, Alexia, had been with me for a couple of months at this point. She has been trying to get over an ex-boyfriend who has hurt her repeatedly. She knows he is not good for her, but a part of her wants to get back together. He, meanwhile, seems to be stuck in this limbo of trying to move forward while his ambivalent tendencies pull him back. Alexia also found herself behaving the same way—attempting to move forward, only to find herself pulling back. They continuously got stuck in the Pursuer–Runner cat-and-mouse chase.

"I texted him this weekend," Alexia confessed.

"What prompted you to do so?" I asked.

"I wished everyone a happy Easter this weekend."

"Do you still have feelings for him?" I cut to the chase.

"I would be lying if I said no," she admitted. "I *do* care about him. I want him to be happy. I want what is best for him. I know it's not great for us to be together, but I think I'd be good for him. It sounds weird, but I think we're a match. I'm so broken and so is he. It doesn't make any sense, I know. I don't want to be with someone who is broken, but I can't cut him off either, because I made a promise that I'd always be there for him. A lot of people think it's a stupid reason to stay in contact with him, but I don't want to break my promises."

After a breakup, we don't just stop caring for someone we once loved, adored, and shared a history with, especially when we know that they also loved us, but can't seem to make up their mind whether to stay or to go. They continuously hurt us time and time again, and it's a frustrated and frustrating love, but feelings can be confusing. Thank God we aren't forced to only rely on our hearts to make decisions; we also have a mind that allows us to think rationally and make wise choices.

Alexia recognizes that she would not *choose* to be with her ex, but she still has feelings for him. There is a reason that part of her wants to be with him; she sees herself as broken and therefore questions why someone who is whole would love her. She feels more comfortable settling for someone who is equally "broken" so that the chances of being abandoned are less. Someone who is "good enough" would be too good for her, she thinks, and might leave her. On top of that, due to the approach-avoidance dynamic in their relationship, each time he pulls away, it reinforces her belief that she is not good enough, while each time he comes back only serves to validate and reward her, as it insinuates that she *is* good enough for him, that she *is* loveable.

Alexia also believes that she is good *for* him—even though they're not good together—because it helps her feel more important. It gives her a sense of purpose and hope that she could help someone. She doesn't want to give up on him, just as she hopes someone who would love her enough not to give up on her. Finally, fixating on him gives her someone else to focus on besides herself. It's easier for her to focus on him than to deal with her own pain and problems.

Cody is Alexia's new boyfriend. He is stable and treats her well, which makes her think that he's too good for her. Intellectually, she wants someone who is good to her and for her, but having someone who treats her well also serves as a constant reminder of her "brokenness." This reminder feeds her doubt that she is not measuring up, that Cody is going to leave her sooner or later. This thought process helps to explain the sabotaging behavior she's demonstrated in many of her relationships.

## Jake

Jake, a new client, is having problems with his girlfriend and came in hoping to find the solution to his relationship issues. Jake has been in a long-distance relationship with his girlfriend for about a year. He wanted his girlfriend to move in with him; he has a stable career, a great place, and he can support her.

"She lives close to her family, but other than that, she doesn't really have a job or much to lose if she moves," he explained. "But the thing is, she has been acting a bit weird the last couple of months. She seems to be pulling away. If I don't try to talk to or text her, then we don't talk. I asked her about it, and she says that's how she is, but I know that's not true. She used to text me all the time."

Naturally, I ask questions to try to better understand his current relationship, as well as inquiring about his relationship history. I also ask if he knew anything about the relationship history of his girlfriend. According to Jake, he has a track record of dating "women with daddy issues," and his girlfriend has always dated "douchebags." Jake states that he and his friends joke about the changes they need to make in order to have a relationship—that they need to "screw up their credit score, lose their job, not have a car, and live in a crappy place" because women "seem to be attracted to that."

"What happens when you meet a woman who's on the same playing field as you are, with all the qualities you just mentioned?" I ask.

"I get intimidated," he confesses.

"So, would you say you date down?"

He contemplates for a moment before admitting, "I date women who need my help so I can feel more superior. I've never thought of it that way, because they are all very attractive; I'm definitely not dating down in that department. And, if I'm doing it, what's to stop her from doing the same thing?"

Jake had connected the dots, and we could both see we had our work cut out for us. He needed to build himself up and see himself for what he's truly worth. He also needed to prevent his fear from standing in the way of a satisfying relationship.

Too often, we let our fears dictate our decisions. We let our past determine our future. But it doesn't have to be this way. I hope you have the courage to change the course of your direction. I understand; when we don't feel good enough about ourselves, we end up with the need to create a dynamic where we're needed. We unconsciously attract people who need some form of rescuing so we can go in and be the hero (or heroine). We enter into relationships out of need, rather than desire. These needs vary; loneliness, feeling empty, wanting someone to make you feel whole, sexually or financially unstable, family obligation, social norms ... the list goes on. This in turn creates an *imbalanced* dynamic, or codependency.

While we need to feel whole, the best way to do so is to address your personal needs yourself before finding a partner who is also whole to share your life with. Remember, it is nice to be needed, but it is even better to be wanted.

## It Doesn't Matter Where You Are in Life

**I want you to honestly evaluate yourself by answering the following questions and giving the reasons why:**

- What's holding me back from getting into a committed relationship or being more intimate with my partner?

- What do I want in a partner?

- Am I independently practicing the qualities I want in my partner?

- What do I have to offer a partner?

- Would I date myself or choose to be in a relationship with myself? Why or why not?

- Am I afraid of losing myself when I'm in a relationship?

- How am I at receiving and giving love?

- Am I focusing on myself as much I focus on my partner?

When you're able to honestly answer these questions, you'll be one step closer to having your ideal partner. When you find yourself, you'll find your ideal love match. Otherwise, you'll feel a need to pick a partner who is inferior to you in some way, so that you can feel superior and try to change your partner. Or you end up feeling inferior and dependent on your partner to take care of you.

One of my clients recently told me that she is getting tired of her boyfriend and is thinking of breaking up with him. She wants someone who is more active; for example, someone who likes hiking after work. She wants her boyfriend to stop eating fast food and not drink every day after work. She's tried to change his habits, but she ends up spending time with him and doing exactly what he does, only to get upset by it later. Yet, when she dated a guy who *was* eating healthy and leading the life that she wanted, she felt like he was too much for her. Seeing his healthy habits made her feel like he was better than she was.

A partnership is like the yoking of two horses to pull the carriage that is your relationship. The horses usually share similarities in strength, height, and agility to work together. So, when you're emotionally at your best, you'll attract someone who's also emotionally healthy. Imagine if you were to yoke a working horse with an injured one. The carriage would not be pulled smoothly, if at all. But when two healthy horses are working together, things are very efficient. When necessary, you can even unyoke them, and each will still be able to operate independently.

We have looked at attachment styles and how they influence our dating life as well as in a relationship. We have discussed the tips and tools necessary to keep your relationship alive. We have also looked at the different stages of a relationship and the evolution necessary for it to thrive. We want independence while yearning for connection and intimacy. I want you to keep the following image of the different stages of a relationship in mind, to help you successfully reach interdependency as a dynamic duo—a relationship in which you have both independence and connection.

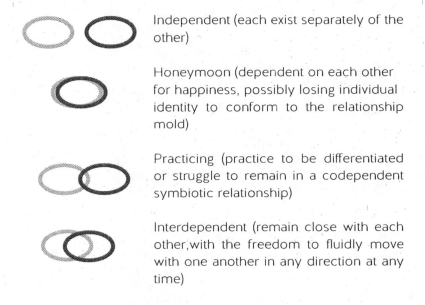

Independent (each exist separately of the other)

Honeymoon (dependent on each other for happiness, possibly losing individual identity to conform to the relationship mold)

Practicing (practice to be differentiated or struggle to remain in a codependent symbiotic relationship)

Interdependent (remain close with each other, with the freedom to fluidly move with one another in any direction at any time)

A dynamic duo is unstoppable together, but each partner remains fiercely self-sufficient and whole when apart. These partners are able to live independently as well as interdependently, working toward supported goals. In other words, each person is as committed to themselves as they are to their partner. A happy relationship is one in which you have enough time together as well as sufficient time away from one another to each have your own life. When you're not spending every waking moment to-gether, you'll be surprised at what each of you can bring to the relationship. My husband once said to me, "You're a mystery," after I shared some trivial information about myself that I can't even remember. At the time, I didn't think much about his state-ment. I wasn't intentionally trying to be mysterious, nor was I withholding information from him, but after all these years, he still finds something new about me. We each have our own lives outside of our relationship.

As I went through the process of writing this book and con-necting all the dots from years of working with my clients and their relationships, I realized that his statement is profound and powerful. After being with a person for a while, we tend to think we know all that we need to know about our partner. We stop looking at them with eyes of wonder and stop being curious about them. We stop trying to find out what gems lie inside their head and heart, not realizing that some of the treasure we've yet to find is newly formed or hidden away.

## ALL THINGS CHANGE

Relationships are ever-changing organisms that mirror the changes within us. These changes occur when we allow ourselves and each other the freedom and room for growth, which is very necessary. I'd imagine most would want to use the most up-to-date computer possible, rather than a slow and outdated version from the 1980s. So why wouldn't you want to have the best of yourself and your partner? It's not possible to have a stagnant relationship that feels alive. Anything that is alive has move-ment. Therefore, changes must be embraced and nurtured for the growth of the relationship.

It can be challenging, of course. You'll feel like you've finally found a rhythm and know how each other works, only for one of you to change for one reason or another. But in a happy relationship, you have to continually develop new rhythms. It's like dancing; you can't just do one dance for every single song. The different stages of your relationship have different beats, and you need to change your rhythm to go with the different tempo. Use Appendix A for maintenance review and tune-up for your relationship.

Too often, I hear couples telling me, "He's changed" or "She's not the person she used to be." I tell each of them the same thing: change is not bad! Whether you met your partner in your twenties, your thirties, or beyond, no one stays the same after twenty, thirty, forty years! We're all still trying to figure things out, usually by trial and error and by making plenty of mistakes. For a person to have remained the same, it means the person hasn't learned or grown at all.

I counsel couples to let go of the image they captured of their partner years ago. That freeze-frame is a snapshot of just a moment in your partner's life. It may look very pretty, but your partner's essence can't be captured by a snapshot. There is so much more to him or her. Your partner must be allowed to change and blossom. It would be more of a concern if a person *didn't* change.

Granted, you'd want the person to change "for the better," though what you consider "better" or "worse" is very subjective. When you're new in a relationship, you tend to project the "good" about yourself, which often leads you to finding and seeing more of the "good" in your prospective partner. Once you've been in a relationship for a while and you've become more comfortable with each other, you're more likely to let your guard down and see more of each other's flaws. When you encounter complicated situations in your relationship, you experience the complexities that different personalities bring to a relationship, as well as having to deal with qualities or characteristics of your partner that you may not like. This tends to heighten your own self-criticalness of your own shortcomings, which in turn fuels the projection of seeing more of the "bad" in your partner. Learn to be more aware and mindful of focusing on what's going right and well instead of the negatives.

Have you ever seen a really old couple together and admired them? I think a lot about where they are in their relationship and how they got there, how they survived what life threw at them, how they manage to lovingly hold onto one another, how they still thrive with each other. We look at these old couples and hope that one day we, too, can have that type of relationship.

What I have found with most of the old couples I've talked to is that they don't question the work that is required in a relationship. Perhaps they've experienced or even struggled through difficult times, but they know that hard work is part of the package. Since you have to do the work no matter what, it is just a question of who you want to work with.

They're also no longer distracted by fear in their relationships. It is true that "perfect love drives out fear," because fear is associated with punishment. These couples live according to one simple goal: to live a happy life and have a happy marriage. They focus on their own wants and needs. They find pleasure in their own hobbies, take pleasure in their own company, and take care of their own business. They also want the same for their partner; they seek to help their partner to achieve this state of interdependence. They mutually appreciate each other, respect one another, accept each other's shortcomings, love unconditionally, and enjoy their partner's company. They strive to keep themselves happy and help their partner to achieve the same.

The good news is, you don't have to wait until you are old to have a perfect love. You do need to understand that relationships naturally evolve and find partners who will fully support that process, helping you to grow and better your relationship. And the only way to help foster growth in a relationship is by working together and allowing each other the personal freedom and independence to have your own identities—to continue to grow into the best version of yourself.

In this process, you'll either grow with each other or you'll grow apart from one another. But once you're convinced of these beliefs, you'll understand that when you're free to leave but choose to stay, the relationship only becomes stronger. It *is* scary to think that our partners can leave at any time; that's what makes love fragile and vulnerable. And naturally, when we're afraid of losing something dear to us, we tend to hold onto it tighter. But the tighter you hold onto your partner, the more suffocating it feels. And like sand, the tighter you grip, the more slips out.

You know the old saying, "If you love something, set it free; if it comes back to you, it's yours forever." I would offer a slight paraphrase: "If you love something, let it go free; if it chooses to stay, you know it's meant to be." At the end of the day, we all want the freedom for autonomy and the acceptance to be who we are as a person.

The best way to love and hold onto your partner is to treat yourself as well as you'd like your partner to treat you. Then, treat your partner as well as you treat yourself and love your partner the way your partner wants to be loved. Remember, loving your partner the way you want to be loved may not be the best-case scenario. You remain two different people, with different wants and needs. We all have different love languages (see Chapter 7), but we all want to be treated with love, trust, and respect.

You are not going to find the perfect partner because you yourself are not perfect. So don't waste your time searching for a perfect love. Instead, spend the time creating it! Rapprochement is as close to perfect as it can be, but you have to *create* that stage. When you're in this stage, the commitment to your relationship is clear. There is a deep understanding, consideration, and respect for your needs as well as your partner's. Your relationship is enhanced by the love actions that are shown on a regular basis. You give genuinely to each other as you reach for a richer level of commitment, intimacy, and vulnerability. You're motivated not by fear, but by love.

At the end of the day, it doesn't matter how broken we are; we all want to feel that we're loved and have someone to love in return. I hope you'd never doubt your sense of self or whether you're good enough to be loved—because you *are*, and you deserve it. Oftentimes, our fear stands in the way—fear of rejection, fear of abandonment, fear of not being good enough—and because of these fears, we deprive ourselves of requited love, that truly beautiful experience. It is the one experience that can only be felt by the heart and sets our soul on fire. When we love and are loved, we can't help but transform.

# Final Thoughts

As humans, we are relational beings. As we go through life, we all want to have someone special to grow old with and to share all that life has to offer. Yet as humans, we take comfort in familiarity. Familiarity is predictable, but it oftentimes holds us back from having the love we desire and achieving the life we want. We fear the unknown and what may seem uncontrollable. It leaves us feeling vulnerable, as though we're not fully in control, especially when it comes to relationships.

For us to grow, we must learn to step out of our comfort zone. To do so in the context of a relationship, however, requires the involvement of another person—someone we have absolutely no control over. Sadly, this fear stops many people from opening up to love.

Of course, no one likes rejection. Rejection hurts. And so we end up depriving ourselves instead of facing the possibility of being rejected. In order for you to conquer your fear, you must first learn to face it. The more you run from your fear, the bigger the fear gets. You can be scared going into it, but go into it all the same. It's the only way to find love.

Intimacy and vulnerability are two faces of the same coin. You can't have one without the other. We all want love and to fall in love, but we're also terrified of the idea of choosing the wrong person for a soulmate. So we wait for the perfect person to come along, or spend our time thinking there may be someone else better suited for us "out there." That perfect soulmate doesn't exist; the real perfect partner is the one we choose to get to know each day, who we work to understand and learn to work with to overcome obstacles.

The trouble is, we live in a society that falsifies what true love looks like. True love is *not* always passionate or romantic. It doesn't always make you want to fall in love because it's not always roses and rainbows. True love is choosing to love when the going gets rough, when your partner is being difficult and you don't like their behavior, but you choose to love them anyway. True love is wanting to be your best so you can give your best to your relationship and partner.

Everlasting love is not an ever-blissful honeymoon. Keep in mind, just like everything else in life, as you grow and change, the dynamics of your relationship also change. Change is good. Don't expect your relationship to stay the same as the day you first met. Allow yourself to go through the necessary stages of the relationship so you can truly understand what it means to be interdependent. Work towards a state where both you and your partner's needs are satisfied, where you're able to work together to find win-win solutions to the never-ending situations that happen in any relationship.

Relationships are hard work, as cliché as it may be. But the work load is lighter when you share. Remember, you're a team. Your enemy is the issues and obstacles that stand in the way of your happiness, not each other. When we're lucky enough to meet a partner who is supportive, understanding, forgiving, and shows you what unconditional love looks like, you can't help but be transformed. And when you have finally chosen a soulmate, don't let your love die. We're in control of our lives and relationships. You're the driver of your destiny. Let love be the motivation of your decisions. Be kind in every action toward yourself and your partner. Nurture your relationship and cherish yourself so that you can have the love of your life and keep your relationship alive.

I hope I've made it easier for you to reach your desired destination with this roadmap of how to better work together. Just remember that knowledge is power, but it can't be achieved without action. Even with my training and expertise in relationships, I still have to put forth a conscious effort to nurture my relationship.

I'm deeply grateful to have finished this book and to be a part of your journey to attract the love of your life and keep your relationship alive. And, if you're willing to share, I'd love to hear your story on how you've applied these practical tools and steps in your journey to find your ideal love match.

# APPENDIX A:
## ANNUAL RELATIONSHIP REVIEW

A healthy and happy relationship needs an investment of time and effort, as well as regular maintenance and tune-up. Below are different aspects of a relationship that can help you do a thorough review of your relationship.

**Looking back at your relationship over this past year, rate how you feel based on the following Likert scale:**

1 – Strongly disagree

2 – Disagree

3 – Somewhat disagree

4 – Neutral or Not sure

5 – Somewhat agree

6 – Agree

7 – Strongly agree

## AFFECTION AND CONNECTION

Affection and connection are the emotional "bank" of a relationship, one which needs consistent deposits. These are positive investments to help keep the relationship going healthy and happy.

___I give you the physical affection you need.

___I'm satisfied with the physical affection you've given me.

___I feel emotionally connected to you.

___I give you emotional affirmation.

___I feel that we're emotionally open to each other.

___I am supportive when you are stressed out or troubled.

___I feel supported by you when I'm stressed out.

___I feel that you're emotionally connected to me.

___I am able to share what's happening in my life with you.

___I feel that you openly share what's going in your life with me.

___I feel intellectually stimulated by you.

___I feel valued and loved by you.

___I give you the love and affection you want.

___I feel that you're emotionally available to me.

___I believe that we're great at showing our love for each other.

## COMMUNICATION

Communication is an important part of any relationship. This category addresses how well you and your partner communicate with each other and listen to one another.

___I feel respected by you.

___I feel that you listen when I talk to you.

___I listen and try to understand your point and perspective.

___I'm able to openly communicate my thoughts and feelings with you.

___I feel validated and understood by you.

___I trust you not to use what I say against me.

___I am not keeping any secrets from you that are vital to our relationship.

___I communicate what is important for me to you.

___I feel that we understand each other.

___You and I communicate with each other on important decisions that needs to be made.

## FUN

Successful relationships take work, but it's not all about work. Couples that play together stay together!

___I have fun with you.

___I feel that you know how to make me smile and cheer me up when I'm down.

___I find ways to make you laugh or we laugh together every day.

___I can be silly with you without worry of being judged.

___I like doing our shared interested and activities together.

___I enjoy your company.

___I feel that you do little things to let me know that you think of me on a regular basis.

___I am reasonably cheerful on most days.

___I feel that you are pleasant and happy around me on
most days.

## GOALS

When you are in a committed relationship, personal goals are as
important as the goals couples have for their relationship.

___I feel that you're supportive of my choices and decisions.

___I feel that you're supportive of my personal development
and my career goals.

___I'm supportive of your dreams and aspirations.

___We have a clear vision or have discussed the plan for our
future together.

___We have the same goals for our relationship.

___I can completely be myself and transparent with you.

___I believe that you help me feel secure in our relationship.

___I have been reliable and consistent for you.

___You're my best friend.

___I would describe our relationship as extremely healthy
and happy.

## HOME

Our environment plays a part in our well-being. Having a happy
home can help couples feel happier with each other.

___Our home environment is generally positive and pleasant.

___I work to maintain a healthy and happy home environment.

___I believe that you work to maintain a positive, pleasant home environment.

___Our home is refuge that I look forward to coming home to at the end of the day.

___I do my fair share of housework.

___Our home is calm and clean.

___I feel that you help with chores to keep the household running smoothly.

___You and I have fairly divided the household responsibilities.

___I believe you help carry the load and are there for me when I need you.

## MONEY

Money is one of the top things that couples argue over. It's not as much about not having money and more the values regarding how to spend the money that causes conflict.

___You and I agree about how to spend money.

___You and I agree about how to save money.

___I feel that you're thoughtful about major expenditures of money and discuss them with me.

___When money is tight, we can discuss our budget without damaging our relationship.

___I feel that money is not tied to power and doesn't change the dynamic of our relationship.

___I have been financially responsible and included you in big purchases.

___We're open and transparent with each other in our financial management.

___I feel that we're equitably contributing (even if there is disparity in income).

___I feel that you have been a good provider, financially.

___I have not completely been financially dependent on you.

## PARENTING

Marital satisfaction tends to drop significantly when children enter the picture. Many couples struggle due to stress related to parenting and the decreased bonding in a relationship. Skip this section if not applicable in your relationship.

___You and I agree on our parenting styles.

___I feel that you carry your fair share in childcare responsibilities.

___You and I are able to openly and respectfully discuss our parenting decisions and discipline with each other.

___You and I don't undermine each other's authority with the children.

___You and I maintain a united front in front of the children. When we disagree, we discuss it with each other afterward.

___You and I have fair and balanced parenting responsibilities when it comes to work and play.

___You and I do not only bond over our children.

___You and I don't argue with each other in front of the children.

___You and I are effective role models for our children.

## PROBLEMS AND DISAGREEMENTS

All couples argue and disagree, but what happens in these moments can have a significant impact on the relationship as a whole, even in times of peace.

___I still feel loved by you when we argue or disagree.

___I don't withhold affection when I'm angry with you.

___You "fight fair" (no name-calling or put downs, dragging up old disagreements, or giving ultimatums)

___I respond to problems constructively (no emotional reactions, thinking before making a decision, not attacking you).

___I feel that you don't shut me down and out (silent treatment, stonewalling).

___I forgive you when you wrong me.

___I believe and accept your apology when you have done something that hurts me.

___When I apologize, you are receptive to it.

___I don't have any built-up resentment towards you.

___I feel that you don't hold grudges against me.

___You and I don't go to bed angry.

___You and I are able to give each other enough space to cool down before coming to our discussion.

___You and I don't have lingering or unresolved arguments that affect our daily interactions.

___You and I collaborate with each other together to find win-win solutions to our problems.

___You and I have been patient with each other.

___You and I don't "sweep things under the rug."

___When we disagree on an issue, I am respectful of you and willingly engage until we have resolved the problem.

___I feel comforted by you when we are faced with problems.

___I feel comfortable raising difficult issues with you.

___I feel that you don't bury important issues.

___I'm able to (and feel safe) tell you what I emotionally need in times of discord.

___You and I are willing to meet each other halfway when necessary.

___You and I see eye-to-eye on major issues.

___Even when we have different opinions, I still feel respected and cared by you.

___You and I are generally able to face and address our issues as they arise.

___I can generally share my concerns and problems with you.

___I feel that you're open to feedback without being defensive.

___You and I are able to successfully resolve the important issues on which we disagree.

## SEX

Sexual intimacy is essential in a relationship, though couples approach sex differently. Healthy sexual communication is vital to understanding each other's needs.

___I am satisfied with the quality of our sex life.

___I am satisfied with the frequency of sex in our relationship.

___I feel safe and secure to express my sexual desires to you.

___You know what I like and dislike to give me a satisfying sexual experience.

___I have made it safe for you to express your sexual desires to me.

___You and I are able to come to an agreement that works for both of us when there is a disparity in the frequency of how often we want sex.

___I feel comfortable letting you know the things I enjoy and don't enjoy about sex.

___You and I are able to recognize that saying "no" to sex at times is not a rejection.

___I'm sexually attracted to you.

___I feel that you sexually woo me.

___I don't feel I'm guilted into having sex with you when I'm
not in the mood.

___I am not worried about you sexually cheating* on me.

___I have been sensitive to your sexual needs.

___Overall, I'm generally satisfied with our sex life.

* Define what sexually cheating means in your relationship

## TIME AND SPACE

A healthy relationship needs to have room for togetherness as
well as individuality. Respect of each other's time and privacy
helps to build trust in a relationship.

___I'm happy with the amount of alone time we each have.

___I like the quality of time we have together.

___I feel that I have an adequate amount of "me" time for
myself.

___I respect your "you" time.

___I feel that you're respectful of my time for family and
friends.

___You and I are supportive and honor each other's separate
interests and hobbies.

___I encourage you to have your own time with family and
friends.

___I feel that you respect my space and privacy, and trust
that I'm not hiding any secrets that are detrimental to our
relationship.

___I don't invade your privacy.

___You and I are supportive of each other's interpersonal relationships outside of our relationship.

___I feel that you put in the effort to plan our "dates" for a good time.

___I have spent as much time with you as you need.

___I'm happy with the time and attention you have given me.

## VALUES

Similar values in a relationship help couples look towards the same direction; however, having respect for differing values is highly important to a healthy relationship.

___You and I share similar values and beliefs.

___I like to continuously learn about myself and grow to be the best version of me.

___I feel that you're open to making changes and improve yourself.

___I feel that you respect my beliefs (political, religion, etc.) even when you disagree with them.

___You and I share similar values when it comes to family and in-laws.

___You and I share similar lifestyles choices (substances, healthy eating, physical exercise, etc.)

## DISCUSSION

Once you and your partner have each completed this inventory in its entirety, sit down together and look at it one area at a time. Acknowledge and validate what each of you have done well, as well as those areas that need improvement. Keep in mind that this exercise is designed to facilitate discussion to improve the quality of your relationship, not as a tool to criticize each other.

**Below are some additional questions to help guide you in your discussion:**

· What are you and your partner doing really well? What helps to make these areas work?

· What specifically excites you about your relationship? What are some specific things that your partner has done to help you feel happy, loved, wanted, and connected that you want to see more of?

· Where are you feeling dissatisfied? Where is your partner feeling dissatisfied?

· What are some specific things each of you can do differently to improve in the areas where you and your partner have expressed dissatisfaction?

· What are you and your partner's hopes for your relationship in the next year?

## SUMMARY:

Right now, I am most happy about:

_____
_____
_____
_____
_____
_____
_____

Right now, I am most concerned about:

_____
_____
_____
_____
_____
_____
_____

My goal for us to work on together in the coming year:

_____
_____
_____
_____
_____
_____
_____

# APPENDIX B:
# NEGOTIATION SHEETS

The following is a negotiation sheet designed to help you and your partner collaborate and smoothly run your household as a team. It helps to have guidelines to help identify our roles and responsibilities in a relationship. You need to target and tackle the issues, not each other. You're responsible and accountable for your part and you need to trust your partner to do the same (so you don't have to "nag").

Directions: On your own, list out all the tasks and chores you can think of that you and your partner do based on each category, and assign a numerical value between 1 and 5 (1 being the simplest or easiest, 5 being most disliked or difficult) to each one. After you complete your list, come together and compare your results. Discuss and (re)negotiate the value for each task so that you both come to an agreement you are happy with. Then divide (and re-divide, if necessary) the work based on your strengths to come to a result with close or equal overall values.

# CURRENT TASKS TABLE

| My Name | | | My Partner's Name | | |
|---|---|---|---|---|---|
| | Assigned Value | Negotiated Value | | Assigned Value | Negotiated Value |
| **DAILY TASKS** | | | | | |
| **WEEKLY TASKS** | | | | | |
| **MONTHLY TASKS** | | | | | |
| **SEASONAL TASKS** | | | | | |

# AGREED TASKS TABLE

| | My Name | My Partner's Name |
|---|---|---|
| DAILY TASKS | | |
| WEEKLY TASKS | | |
| MONTHLY TASKS | | |
| SEASONAL TASKS | | |

# READING LIST

Bader, Ellyn, and Pearson, T. Peter. *In Quest of the Mythical Mate*. New York: Brunner/Mazel, Inc., 1988.

Bowen, M. *Family therapy in clinical practice*. New York: Jason Aronson, 1978."

Bowlby, John, and Ainsworth, Mary. *The origins of attachment theory*. Developmental Psychology, Vol 28(5), 1992, 759-775.

Carrere, S., and Gottman, J. M. *Predicting divorce among newlyweds from the first three minutes of a marital conflict discussion*. Family Process, 38(3), 1999, 293-301.

Chapman, Gary. *The 5 Love Languages*. Chicago, IL: Northfield Publishing, 1992.

Fisher, Helen. *Why Him? Why Her?* New York: Henry Holt and Company, 2009.

Fraley, R. C., Waller, N. G., & Brennan, K.A. *An item-response theory analysis of self-report measures of adult attachment*. Journal of Personality and Social Psychology, 78, 2000, 350-365.

Gottman, John. *Why Marriages Succeed or Fail*. New York: Simon & Schuster, 1994.

Gottman, J.M., and Levenson, R.W. *A two-factor model for predicting when a couple will divorce: Exploratory analysis using 14-year longitudinal data*. Family Process, 41(1), 2002, 83-96.

Hazan, Cindy and Shaver Phillip. *Romantic Love Conceptualized as an Attachment Process*. Journal of Personality and Social Psychology, 52(3), 1987, 511-524.

Kübler-Ross, Elisabeth. *On Death and Dying*. New York: The Macmillan Company, 1969.

Levine, Amir and Heller, Rachel. *Attached: The New Science of Adult Attachment and How It Can Help You Find and Keep Love*. New York: Penguin Group, 2012.

Pham, T. Shaelyn. *The Joy of Me*. Hatherleigh Press, 2016.

Salter Ainsworth, D. Mary, Blehar, C. Mary, Waters, and Wall, N. Sally. *Patterns of Attachment*. Routledge: Taylor & Fancis Group, 2015.

Skowron, A. Elizabeth and Friedlander, L. Myrna. *The Differentiation of Self Inventory: Development and Initial Validation*. Journal of Counseling Psychology, vol. 45, No. 3 (1998): 234-246.

The Bible (New International Version)